1·95

MALIA

By the staff of Editions Berlitz

Preface

A new kind of travel guide for the jet age—Berlitz has packed all you need to know about Malta and Gozo into this compact and colourful book, one of an extensive series on the world's top tourist areas.

Like our phrase books and dictionaries, this book fits your pocket—in both size and price. It also aims to fit your travel needs:

- It combines easy reading with fast facts: what to see and do, where to shop, what to eat.

- An authoritative A-to-Z "blueprint" fills the back of the book, giving clear-cut answers to all your questions, from "What time do the banks open?" to "Is the water safe to drink?"—plus how to get there, when to go and what to budget.

- Easy-to-read maps in full colour pinpoint the sights you'll want to see.

In short, this handy guide will help you enjoy your trip to Malta and Gozo. From the palaces of the Knights of St. John to the eerie temples of Ġgantija, from Valletta's cheerful *karrozzin* surreys to the golden beach of Mellieħa Bay, Berlitz tells you clearly and concisely what it's all about.

Let your travel agent help you choose a hotel.

Let a restaurant guide help you find a good place to eat.

But to decide "What should we do today?" travel with Berlitz.

Area specialist: Suzanne Patterson
Photography: Ken Welsh
Layout: Hanspeter Schmidt
We are grateful to Mr. and Mrs. Joseph Arrigo, Mr. and Mrs. Robert Hammond, Mr. and Mrs. James Pettigrew and Mr. J. G. Vassallo for their help in the preparation of this book. We would also like to thank the National Tourist Organization of Malta and Air Malta for their valuable assistance.
Cartography: Falk-Verlag, Hamburg.

Contents

Maps: The Maltese Islands p. 9, Malta p. 27, Valletta—Town Centre p. 31, Valletta and Suburbs p. 45, Mdina and Rabat p. 51, Gozo and Comino p. 71, Victoria (Rabat) p. 75.
Cover: Bobbing boats in St. Julian's Bay.

How to use this guide

If time is short, look for items to visit which are printed in bold type in this book, e.g. **National Museum of Archaeology.** Those sights most highly recommended are not only given in bold type but also carry our traveller symbol, e.g. **St. John's Co-Cathedral.**

Malta and the Maltese

The strategic position of Malta, Gozo and Comino have made the islands of the Maltese archipelago a crossroads of history and often a bone of contention. But for the jet-age traveller, these Mediterranean islands, only 60 miles south of Sicily and 220 miles north of the deserts of Libya, are a good place for a beach holiday—with the added attraction of dozens of sights and monuments from a fascinating past.

Approached by air or sea, Malta seems arid and austere. But as you get nearer, the landscape of the main island softens with a special beauty. A pink-and-ochre rocky surface is filled with free-stone fences rambling over pockets of greenery, dotted with dozens of church belfries. In cobalt-blue harbours and tiny inlets, little multi-coloured *luzzu* fishing boats—with the fierce eyes of Osiris painted on their bows to ward off the evil eye—bob next to yachts, cruise-ships and mammoth oil tankers.

Inland, the countryside is full of contrasts. The scene is biblical—flat-topped houses against a sere background. Yet, at the time of the spring flowering,

the barren hills burst into colour. Herds of goats vie for road space with big cars; 20th-century ideas mix strangely with religious traditions. On this pretty and paradoxical island, the phone boxes could be London's, if they weren't painted blue, and the pizzas seem Italian, but they couldn't be

6

more genuinely Maltese, as you'll soon find out.

Valletta, the capital city, is ringed by fortresses. In the past they provided the islanders with protection. Today their architecture is admired by visitors from all over the world. For while there are still factories making small components

Malta in a nutshell: man and beast till the land beneath skyline of church towers and windmills.

or jeans or tinned tomato paste, one of Malta's biggest industries is tourism. New hotels line the bays and beaches north-west of Valletta; most of **7**

Malta in a Minute

Some of the information given below can be found in different sections of our guide, but for your convenience it is gathered together here for a quick briefing.

Geography	Malta, Gozo and Comino comprise the Republic of Malta, 60 miles south of Sicily in the Mediterranean Sea with an area of 122 square miles. Population 330,000. Travel time from London, about 3 hours Heathrow to Luqa.
Climate	Good months for visiting are April, May, June, October and November. July and August are hot. January is the coldest month.
Government	Became a democratic republic within the British Commonwealth on December 13, 1974.
Religion	Roman Catholic.

the year the islands bask in sunny holiday weather and in summer the temperature can soar. Wherever you are, the tempting dark-blue Mediterranean is never far away and always ready to refresh you.

The main island is just 95 square miles (one-sixth the size of greater London) and you can travel easily from place to place, by car, bus or taxi. Gozo is even smaller, only 26 square miles, and remains a rustic, unspoilt outpost. Between Malta and Gozo, tiny Comino has one square mile, one hotel and a handful of residents and tourists.

The total population of the island nation is estimated to be about 330,000 with 300,000 on Malta, 30,000 on Gozo. People have lived on the islands since Neolithic times, well over 5,000 years ago. Colonized by almost every Mediterranean power—from the Phoenicians and the Spanish to the Knights of the Order of St. John and the British—the country became an independent nation in 1964.

From these different roots, the Maltese people have emerged. For the most part, they are sturdy, dark-haired and olive-skinned, almost all great swimmers and good sailors. Visitors are invariably impressed by the islanders who are among the most polite and good-natured in the world. They are proud and fun-loving and know how to laugh at themselves as well as with everybody else. Work gets

THE MALTESE ISLANDS

done—but it's never taken too seriously.

Everyone speaks Malti, a language related to Arabic, with some Italian and a little French thrown in. It's an exotic tongue for foreigners. The Malti for "street", for example, is *triq*. With many consonants, the pronunciation is difficult. *Xewkija* on Gozo is pronounced "shoo-KEE-yah". But tourists have few language problems, as English is taught in the schools. Almost all Maltese speak it fairly well.

The addition of the English language and certain Anglo-Saxon customs and food to Mediterranean ways has given rise to a unique local style. Read the hand-painted signs of Malta for a vocabulary lesson: "The Up-to-Date Garage", "The Still-Alive Bar", "The Intact Boutique", "The Perfection Confectionery".

Malta became Christian after St. Paul was shipwrecked there in A.D. 60. Today, in Rabat, you can visit the spot where the apostle is said to have stayed. Religion is taken seriously and there are wayside chapels everywhere. Each town and parish is fiercely proud of its church. Keeping up with the Joneses in Malta means keeping up with the neighbouring town's church and building a bigger, better one next time round.

The explosions you hear on weekends all summer long come from religious festivities or *festi*. These are well-attended events with parades, bands and fireworks. The churches take out their best silver objects and damask trappings; the **9** streets are decorated with huge statues of saints and are thronged with people. You'll hear Holy Masses, but sense a carnival atmosphere as well.

Malta has produced several good local artists, though some of the finest paintings found in the islands were done by the Italians Caravaggio and Mattia Preti. More contemporary are the sculptures of Antonio Sciortino. Many of his figures, full of grace and movement, can be seen on display. Local artisans' work, hand-blown glass, silver filigree, weaving, lace and pottery are undergoing an enthusiastic revival.

The islands are full of fascination and fun. The mystery becomes palpable as you wander through the prehistoric ruins of Ħaġar Qim or visit Gozo's Ġgantija, with the wind whistling eerily around you. No one can fully explain the strange lost civilizations that built them there.

But nobody will be needed to help you enjoy the pleasures of the warm sandy beaches, the rock bathing and myriad water sports. A surprise lies around every corner: children playing with a pet goat; an ancient bare-footed crone clicking her bobbins to produce spiderwebs of lace; a *karrozzin* (surrey with

a fringe on top); or a *dgħajsa* (a colourful water-taxi) plying its trade.

Whatever your interests—whether archaeological, artistic, religious or sporting—you'll find something to satisfy you in Malta. And nobody will criticize if you just want to soak up the sun at a swimming pool with the prospect of a leisurely lunch by the sea later on.

Mediterranean waves wash the golden sands of Gozo's Ramla beach, big enough for holiday throngs; ginger cat, left, surveys Valletta.

A Brief History

Often ruled, never truly dominated, the Maltese islands command a striking place in European history. Their past is marked by violence, intrigue and courage shown during battles fought over the centuries for the strategically situated islands. Eyed covetously, ruled by many different factions and nations, Malta has been called "a palimpsest of history" —meaning an original manuscript erased and re-written over many times.

But long before recorded history, a civilization of a kind had dawned on Malta. In the Stone, Copper and Bronze ages, the island boasted an organized society, capable of producing quite complex architectural structures.

The first settlers—probably peasant-farmers—had crossed over from Sicily sometime between 5000 and 4000 B.C. Fascinating traces of these early inhabitants and the generations that followed them can still be seen all over the islands. Their driving force was a primitive religious cult probably related to death and fertility.

Profile of fishing boats, colour of stone are distinctively Maltese.

You can visit many of the prehistoric sites. One extraordinary underground complex of cave-like tombs on Malta is at Paola. Called the Hypogeum, and dating back to about 2400 B.C., the elliptical-shaped rooms and passages served as a temple. The basic architectural forms found here also appear above-ground in enormous enterprises, such as Ġgantija on Gozo or Ħaġar Qim on Malta.

Some of the best of these prehistoric buildings were built during the Tarxien era and were a stunning feat of construction for such supposedly unsophisticated people. But then, around 2000 B.C., the whole temple-building civilization disappeared. The mystery has been variously explained as being caused by plague or—more likely—by overpopulation, for what the land could produce, aggravated by lack of rain, was insufficient to meet the islanders' needs.

The next wave of immigrants appears to have come from southern Italy. This group, who used the Tarxien temples as a burial ground, were known as "the Cemetery People". They were followed by others, who built a defensive wall at Borġ in-Nadur, and settled in fortified villages. **13**

The Great "Cart Track" Mystery

Parts of the stony land of Malta and Gozo are criss-crossed with prehistoric "cart tracks". They are not always of the same width, and were probably not even made by carts.

The tracks have been found all over village sites and seem to have been used for some kind of vehicle. The ancient buggies were probably "slide carts", with two shafts attached to a draught animal which dragged two stones attached by a crossbar behind it. On the bar might have been placed building materials, agricultural produce, or other loads.

Carthaginians and Romans

Recorded Maltese history began around the 9th century B.C., with the arrival of the Phoenicians. Later, in the 6th century B.C., came traders from the Phoenician colony of Carthage. A brilliant Mediterranean people, their colonization was to last for centuries.

Another strong influence in Maltese history was that of the Greeks. Although they never colonized the nation, the presence of many coins and inscriptions suggests that they visited Malta between the 6th and 7th centuries B.C.

Malta's strategic significance came back into the spotlight during the Punic Wars (the three wars in the 3rd and 2nd centuries B.C. between Phoenician Carthage and Rome). The island was fought over by the great powers but it finally fell to the Roman consul Tiberius Sempronius in 218 B.C.

The Carthaginians had built their central capital on a hill-top, where Mdina is now, and the Romans took this over as their base, fortifying it and building luxurious villas in and around it. You can still see a good reconstruction of one of these typical Roman houses, between Mdina and Rabat.

One of Malta's most important historical events happened during Roman rule. In A.D. 60, St. Paul and St. Luke were shipwrecked on Malta, somewhere around the area now known as St. Paul's Bay. Paul's preaching in Jerusalem and Caesarea had caused such an outcry among the religious leaders that the Romans had arrested him, partly for his own safety. During the subsequent enquiry, Paul, a Roman citizen, appealed to Caesar for justice and it was when he and Luke were travelling as prisoners from Caesarea to Rome that the ship foundered on the rocks of Malta.

Street corner shrine amidst typical Valletta balconies: delicately sculpted stone statue of Paul the apostle honours shipwrecked saint.

For a whole winter they stayed in a cave at Mdina-Rabat, and St. Paul preached the Gospel. His message and the miracles that happened in his presence were sufficient to convert the Roman Governor, Publius, who subsequently became the first Bishop of Malta and was later martyred and canonized. Despite different governments and the spreading of Islam by the Arabs, Malta has remained fundamentally Christian from St. Paul's day to this.

The Dark Ages and Arab Rule

As the Roman Empire declined, Malta's history becomes obscure. In 870 the Arabs became the new rulers. Although they tolerated Christianity, many islanders seem to have emigrated or to have become Moslem. At that time, slavery was a big business, and trading was carried on by both Maltese and Arabs. The victims were mainly Christians from neighbouring countries.

Two centuries of Arab rule left an indelible impression on **15**

What's in a Name?
The origin of the word Malta has been guessed at by a number of different people. But finally, the two most plausible solutions are that it could either be a corruption of the word *malat* (Phoenician for port of safe harbour) or could come from the Greek *meli* (honey), a famous product of the Maltese islands in early times.

Gozo (or Għawdex, pronounced "Ow-dehsh" in Maltese) probably comes from the Greek *gaudos*, which is derived in turn from the Phoenician word for a small round boat.

the island, particularly on the language. The Arabs also introduced the cultivation of cotton and citrus fruit, which became very important to the economy. Malta was now a prosperous Mediterranean trading nation.

But quarrelling factions among the rulers soon made the island ripe for conquest— this time by Count Roger the Norman, son of Tancred de Hauteville, in 1090–91. Roger, who had inherited a principality in southern Italy from his father, wanted to ensure the defence of Sicily by controlling Malta. His conquest **16** of St. Paul's Bay and, later,

Mdina was relatively easy and Malta became part of the Kingdom of Sicily. The new ruler was fairly liberal and let the islanders govern themselves by local councils. Moslems were tolerated, and the Christian church was encouraged to renew and expand itself.

During the Crusades, Malta was a key link in Christianity's line of defence against the Moslems, even though Maltese Moslems were still living there.

After being attached to Sicily, Malta passed into the hands of the Swabians and then to the French king's (Louis IX's) brother, Charles of Anjou. The French remained in power until being ousted by Peter I of Aragon in 1282, when the islands became an Aragonese possession.

Under the uneasy joint Spanish-Sicilian rule, Malta was exploited by overseas noblemen only interested in the country as a source of revenue. The Maltese themselves worked at trading, slaving and piracy to provide taxes and income for the owners.

By the 15th century, local self-government had reached a certain level of maturity with an administrative body known as the Università governing and distributing food supplies. Tired of exploitation by foreign nobility, the Università managed to raise a substantial sum of money to bring Malta into a more secure relationship with Spain. Thus, in 1428, the Spanish King Alfonso V declared Malta "reunited in perpetuity" to the Crown, which administered the island directly, without the landlords.

Meanwhile, the islands were continually and repeatedly raided by Berbers, Turks and Saracens. By the 16th century, the morale of the country was sinking and the economy was on the decline.

The Knights' Arrival

But other developments in the Mediterranean area were already taking place that would change Maltese fortunes. In the early 16th century, Sultan Suleiman the Magnificent and the Turks more or less ruled the seas in the name of Islam. They had long harassed the Knights of the Order of St. John on Rhodes, and finally occupied that island on New Year's Day, 1523, after a six-month siege. This left the knights homeless.

The courageous Grand Master, Philippe Villiers de l'Isle-Adam, led his soldiers to Sicily and Italy. But Europe's loyalties were divided between Francis I of France and Charles V, Holy Roman Emperor and King of Spain and Sicily. Finding a permanent settlement for the knights was a thorny problem.

After seven years of negotiations, the knights reluctantly agreed to take over Malta and the island was granted to the Order nearly rent-free—in exchange for the token payment of one falcon a year (the famous "Maltese falcon", though not much to do with the film of that name). So, in 1530, the Grand Master with his 4,000 men moved into Malta.

Though the islanders were uneasy about the new occupants at first, their rights and privileges were respected. The knights built fortifications and living quarters in Birgu (later called Vittoriosa) and generally strengthened the area that is now known as Valletta (the Sceberras peninsula between Grand and Marsamxett harbours). The capital became the new focus of interest on Malta and attention was taken away from the old town of Mdina.

The Grand Master Villiers de l'Isle-Adam died in 1534, was succeeded by several others and finally by Jean Parisot de la Valette in 1557. His name was to become famous in the island's history.

The Knights of St. John

The full title of the Order was the Knights Hospitalers of St. John of Jerusalem. The Order was founded in Jerusalem in the 11th century when some Italian merchants obtained permission from the Moslem caliph to set up a hospice for Christian pilgrims. The calling of the brothers was principally to care for the sick, but in time the emphasis shifted from the medical and religious arms of the Order to the knights' military task: that of fighting the infidel.

In 1187 the knights were driven from Jerusalem by Saladin and had to move on to Acre and then Cyprus, retreating finally to the island of Rhodes in 1308. Though the Turks laid siege to the island several times, it wasn't until 1522, when they were attacked by Suleiman (the Magnificent), that the knights were forced to surrender.

The knights took vows of poverty, chastity and obedience and were divided into three main grades: Knights of Justice (bona fide aristocrats from all over Europe, who wore the 8-pointed cross, now called the Maltese cross), Sergeants at Arms (who acted as both soldiers and nurses), and Chaplains (who worked in the hospitals and churches).

The knights were grouped under eight *langues* or "tongues", three of them French, as France was divided in the 13th century into France, Provence and Auvergne. The other *langues* were Aragon, Castille, Italy, Germany and England. After the Reformation in the 16th century the English *langue* had ceased to exist. A joint *langue* of England and Bavaria was set up in 1784. Each *langue* was headed by a *pilier*, who had a set function; thus the *pilier* of Italy was Grand Admiral; the *pilier* of Provence was financial and ordnance manager; the *pilier* of France was head of the Order's hospitals, etc.

In the 16th century, the knights had over 650 *commanderies* in Europe, and huge estates all over the continent. Their supreme head was the Grand Master, elected for life, and subject only to the Pope.

As the years progressed the knights lapsed into careless and dissolute ways. Discipline became lax, corruption crept in and internal dissensions added to the failing powers of the Order. A fitting tribute to the original motives of the Hospitalers is the St. John Ambulance Association; the Order of St. John is still a sovereign Order with headquarters in Rome.

Philippe Villiers de l'Isle-Adam led knights to Malta in 1530.

For years, Turks had been attacking the knights on Malta, determined to take possession of the tiny island for its strategic position astride the Mediterranean sea routes. Another menace to the peace was a North-African pirate called Dragut. He had his own designs on Gozo, devastating it in 1546 and taking over 6,000 Gozitans away as slaves in 1551. Dragut then joined the Turks, adding his own forces to the growing threat to Christendom all over the Mediterranean.

The Great Siege

Suleiman the Magnificent decided the time was ripe for Islam to strike in a big way and began an unprecedented build-up of troops. This was reported to Grand Master de la Valette, who frantically sent out an ap- **19**

peal for assistance to friendly quarters, but no help came, and on May 19, 1565, a Turkish fleet of 138 galleys disembarked 38,000 troops at Marsaxlokk Bay.

This looked like a disaster for de la Valette and his 600 knights, with only 9,000 troops and eight galleys at his disposal. The Turks—under Admiral Piali and Mustapha Pasha—felt sure they would win. Among their troops was a special corps of 4,000 janissaries—a group trained for fighting and killing only.

The knights carried out one of the most valiant defences in all history, though things

The Great Siege: fresco depicts brave standoff of forces in 1565.

went badly throughout. Fort St. Elmo was finally overrun in a battle fought to the last man. After the massacre, the Turks tied the knights' corpses to crosses and set them afloat in the Grand Harbour, to the horror of the others opposite at Birgu. Dragut the pirate was also killed in this battle, struck by a cannonball. He was to be sorely missed by the Islamic forces. The place where he fell is called Dragut point, on Marsamxett Harbour, opposite Fort St. Elmo.

De la Valette reinforced his defences at Birgu and Senglea. The critical moment of the siege had come, and Queen Elizabeth of England instructed prayers to be said in all the churches of her realm. All Christendom worried, but nobody came to help. Throughout the terrible summer of 1565, as heat, disease and dwindling food supplies plagued them, the two sides battled on in their holy war. The whole Maltese population fought along with the knights, fiercely resisting the invaders.

Despite all their troops, their explosives and their dedication, the Turks were gradually worn down. The fact that there was often disagreement between their two top commanders didn't help matters. In one assault alone, the Turks lost 2,500 men.

But the knights, too, had their problems, losing both irreplaceable men and strategic positions to the Turks. Even de la Valette (though he was 72) threw himself violently into battle. His courageous action came at a low moment for the knights and was a great encouragement to his men.

Outside help for the Maltese and knights finally arrived with the Sicilian Viceroy, Garcia de Toledo, who brought reinforcements he had mustered with difficulty after renewed pleas from de la Valette.

By late summer, the Turks had run out of supplies, firm leadership and spirit and on September 8th, 1565, the siege was lifted and what was left of the attack force sailed away; most historians reckon well over two-thirds of their forces were lost. There was general rejoicing in Malta, though the main island had been devastated.

With money from the knights and European powers, plans were quickly drawn up for a new city between the two long harbours, in the area known as Sceberras. The knights obtained the help of Laparelli, the Pope's own architect. The cost was astronomical, but the kings of Europe sent generous gifts to support the project. Named after the courageous de la Valette, Valletta was born.

During the two final centuries of the knights' rule, Malta grew and prospered. Trading activities were renewed and developed, and there was a surge of grandiose building projects. After Laparelli, Gerolamo Cassar—a Maltese architect—took over, and is responsible for much of the way Valletta looks today: a harmonious early Baroque style tempered by a classic approach.

At about this time Mediterranean traders were beginning to feel the effects of the discovery of the alternative route (round the Cape of Good Hope) to the riches of India; and by the 18th century, with the emphasis of the main trading activities turned towards America, the prosperity of former years waned. The Order, too, was declining into a somewhat dissolute middle age. With the French Revolution of 1789, and the downfall of the aristocracy and church of France, the knights suffered another blow, losing a great deal of prestige—and revenue (a huge proportion had been French).

Enter Napoleon
In 1798, while planning his Empire-building projects, Napoleon came to the same conclusion other military minds had reached over the centuries. Realizing that Malta would be a valuable strategic outpost, he sailed into Marsaxlokk harbour on June 10, 1798, and went to Valletta, where he presented the knights with an ultimatum to pack up and leave. Where others had failed, Napoleon succeeded. The Grand Master, de Hompesch, meekly gave in,

and after centuries of residence the world's most famous military Order duly departed.

Napoleon started energetically promulgating new laws, but then he also left, only six days after the knights. The subsequent two-year reign of the French was nasty and unpleasant. They came as conquerors and looters and were highly unpopular with the people and the Church. This encouraged the Maltese to embark on an insurrection that lasted on and off for 18 months. With troops sent by the King of Naples joining in on the Maltese side, and that scourge of the French, Admiral Nelson, patrolling the Mediterranean, Napoleon's soldiers were forced to capitulate in 1800. In 1802, the Treaty of Amiens formally restored Malta to the Order of St. John.

Great Britain, now approaching the height of her sea-power, had meanwhile become aware of Malta's value as a naval base. After informally occupying the islands and administering them through Alexander Ball, Britain finally had her possession of the territory formally recognized by the Treaty of Paris in 1814, and again during the Congress of Vienna in the following year. Thus, Malta entered a period of British rule that was to last until 1964. Even then, British forces were to stay on, using bases in the islands, until 1979.

British Rule

During the next century, the population of the islands grew considerably, while the economy fluctuated. Agricultural changes introduced by the British included potato farming (which flourished) and the silk industry (which soon died). Cotton production, once all-important, declined. New water sources were found and vineyards expanded.

In 1813, when a plague epidemic killed a fifth of the population, Sir Thomas Maitland became governor. Sir Thomas brought autocratic rule to Malta, and was nicknamed "King Tom". He dismissed the traditional local, self-governing body of the Università, and made sweeping reforms to bring Malta into line with the British judiciary system—though old practices often continued.

The installation of bases, shipbuilding and harbour facilities proved a boon to the Maltese economy. By 1880 the Grand Harbour in Valletta was a major entrepôt, with many ships calling at the port. Thereafter, however, as the size

The Language Dilemma

When the British arrived on the scene, the people's spoken language was Maltese, as it is today. But the knights had used Italian for official matters, and the middle and upper classes continued to use it, especially in the courts and for business. Sir Thomas Maitland declared that English should be used, but years of confusion followed before English was finally adopted as the official administrative language in 1921.

During British rule, English was taught in schools—as it has been since independence. Most Maltese speak good English.

of the ships became larger and outside investment declined, competition from other ports increased and Malta's importance as a centre of trade diminished.

During the 19th century, a succession of constitutions gave the Maltese varying degrees of autonomy. Then local riots in 1919 brought about changes, resulting in the new Constitution of 1921. The Maltese became responsible for their own internal affairs, with Great Britain, through its governor, retaining control of foreign affairs and imperial matters.

The Second Great Siege

Malta's finest hour in modern times was undoubtedly the heroic defence of the islands in World War II, which earned the George Cross. A vital Allied base, Malta was a haven for aircraft and ships. It not only helped to block the deployment of Italy's naval forces, but also threatened Axis supply routes between the European continent and the forces (above all, those under General Rommel) that were

A pigeon crowns statue of Queen Victoria before National Library. Malta became independent in 1964.

operating in North Africa. It was no surprise, therefore, when Italian and Italian-based German bombers and fighters attacked Malta in 1941 in a fierce blitz that marked the start of a siege that was to last for months, until November 1942.

through to the beleaguered and suffering islands with a major convoy carrying urgently needed military and civilian supplies. This perilous operation was code-named "Pedestal".

In August 1942, fourteen supply ships and a tanker moved with naval and air cover through the straits of Gibraltar. There were a succession of fierce Italian air attacks on the convoy. Several ships were sunk and the tanker *Ohio*, a key ship, with its especially important cargo of oil, was badly damaged.

But despite a very rough five days of bombardment, on August 15th, the *Ohio* was finally towed into the Grand Harbour. The assembled crowds wept and cheered; Malta was saved. By November, when a major new Allied landing took place in Morocco and Rommel's forces were retreating from the frontiers of Egypt, following the battle of El Alamein, Malta could begin to see the victory that its own courage had helped make possible.

But the price of freedom had been high: thousands of Maltese had been killed or seriously injured. It was only fitting, concluded Churchill, that Malta be awarded Great Britain's highest honour for civil courage—the George Cross.

As Rommel advanced in Egypt in the spring of 1942, enemy air attacks were stepped up, and in March and April the islands were subjected to more than twice the weight of bombs falling in London during any year of the war.

That summer, life grew unbearably hard on Malta, and the people had to carry on in near-starvation conditions. The government in London therefore decided to take the huge risk of trying to force a way

Independence

In 1942, Great Britain provided Malta with £30 million towards reconstruction, and a new constitution granted the islands self-government within the Commonwealth. Various plans for the complete transfer of power met with difficulties both in Great Britain and Malta, but finally, on September 21, 1964, Malta became officially independent. It had a Governor-General and a Parliament of fifty members. In 1971, the Labour Party was voted into power with Dom Mintoff as Prime Minister.

The Union Jack was lowered for good on April 1, 1979, when the British forces which had remained in bases on Malta finally pulled out. The occasion also marked the end of British financial aid and terminated several years of friction between Britain and Dom Mintoff, who treated the withdrawal as Freedom Day.

But on both sides, British and Maltese, there were those who were sad at the parting. Although the Maltese are proud of their independence, they retain a fund of goodwill towards the many British residents on Malta and Gozo and the thousands of Britons who happily spend their holidays there.

Where to Go

As the longest distance in Malta (from south-east to north-west) is only just over 16 miles, it is very easy to see a great deal in a short time. But quality is better than quantity, and the real advantage of Malta's tiny size is that you can take your time at places of interest and plan your sightseeing in any order you like, depending on whether you're in the mood for churches, villages, prehistoric sites, boat trips, beaches or just a shopping expedition in Valletta.

Thousands of years of dramatic history are compressed into these few square miles. You'll have to fight off many a tempting distraction if you hope to catch up with all the island's significant sights. In this book, we start with Valletta and suburbs, move on to Mdina and Rabat and then visit the south-east and north-west coasts. The special section on Malta's prehistoric temples gathers all the information on this ancient and mysterious culture into one chapter for handy reference. Finally, we give a complete summary of where to go on Gozo. But first, the city that has been at the centre of Malta's turbulent history…

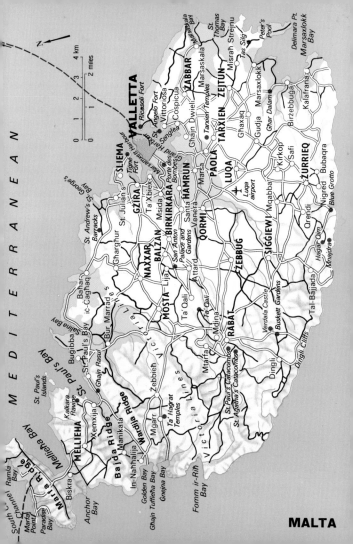

MALTA

Valletta

"That splendid town, quite like a dream", wrote Sir Walter Scott. When you see Valletta, especially from the air or sea late on a dazzling summer's afternoon, you'll agree with him. The light plays games with the city's bright stone bastions and buildings, turning it into a place of enchantment that seems to float on an indigo sea.

It was not always this way. Mdina, the walled inland city, had been the capital of Malta from pre-Roman times until the Great Siege of 1565. But Grand Master Jean Parisot de la Valette saw the defensive possibilities of the Sceberras peninsula and his imagination was fired. After the knights' victory, plans were laid to build a capital town with invulnerable fortifications. The sharply hog-backed ridge with its two great natural harbours, Marsamxett on one side and the Grand Harbour on the other,

was the perfect place for a fortified town. So it was that in 1566, despite the enormous cost anticipated, work was begun by Francesco Laparelli, who had served as architect to Cosimo de' Medici and Pope Pius IV.

Laparelli is said to have masterminded the entire city plan in a mere three days, and two years later, when he left, Gerolamo Cassar (his Maltese assistant) took over and kept to the original conception.

The new city was constructed quickly but intelligently. Around the base, a solid line of stone curtains and bastions made it virtually impregnable. The uniformity of the grid-shaped street plan led it to be called a "city built for gentlemen". Water supply problems were solved in the 17th century

Woman in black, left, peers over laundry at Valletta life; flower stall adds colour and fragrance.

when Grand Master Alof de Wignacourt ordered the construction of an aqueduct to carry water from springs near Mdina to the new capital and gardens were added near the fortifications.

Valletta suffered from merciless bombing in World War II, but it was a victorious and courageous Maltese people who wept with joy when the blockade was broken in 1942. They are proud of their city, and have kept its original charms intact. It is a city with a soul, where everyone Maltese, from aristocrat to simple fisherman, walks with his head held high.

Around the Old Town

The best way to visit Valletta is on foot. Driving is inadvisable, as the streets are narrow and many are closed to traffic. Sunset is a good moment for a walk round, when shadows are cooling the streets, and the town is seething with strollers out for the evening social hour known as the *passeggiata*.

Enter the city after the roundabout bus terminal and Triton Fountain through the modern City Gate built in postwar style, with an arcade and complex of shops on either side. Directly ahead is the main Republic Street, formerly

Fortifications Galore

In the 16th century, one of the first things to be done after constructing a new city was to put up fortifications of one kind or another. Valletta, Floriana and their surrounding suburbs contain enough bastions, curtains, forts, towers, cavaliers, ravelins, ramparts, trenches, ditches, walls and other defensive structures to send any budding military engineer into frissons of ecstasy.

The typical zig-zag bastion provided the most effective defence. The nearer the enemy approached the bastion, the easier it became for the defenders to fire on the attackers along the flanks. Defences were thus "strengthened" without a real increase in arms, ammunition or men.

The best way to appreciate Valletta's fortifications (completed between 1566 and 1570) is to walk along the tops of them. To go around completely once takes about two hours (allowing for time to stop and admire the views).

called Kingsway. It is closed to all motor traffic. Parallel to it on the right is the second principal artery, Merchants Street. Both streets run straight on for just under a mile, to Fort St. Elmo at the end of the peninsula.

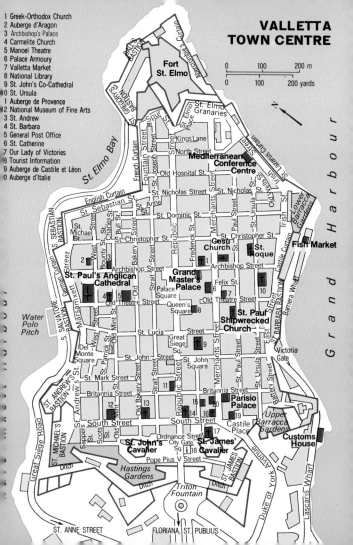

VALLETTA
TOWN CENTRE

1 Greek-Orthodox Church
2 Auberge d'Aragon
3 Archbishop's Palace
4 Carmelite Church
5 Manoel Theatre
6 Palace Armoury
7 Valletta Market
8 National Library
9 St. John's Co-Cathedral
10 St. Ursula
11 Auberge de Provence
12 National Museum of Fine Arts
13 St. Andrew
14 St. Barbara
15 General Post Office
16 St. Catherine
17 Our Lady of Victories
18 Tourist Information
19 Auberge de Castile et Léon
20 Auberge d'Italie

Fort
St. Elmo

Mediterranean
Conference
Centre

Fish Market

Gesù
Church

St.
Roque

St. Paul's Anglican
Cathedral

Grand
Master's
Palace

St. Paul
Shipwrecked
Church

Water
Polo
Pitch

Great
Siege
Sq.

Parisio
Palace

Upper
Barracca
Gardens

St. John's
Cavalier

St. James'
Cavalier

Customs
House

Hastings
Gardens

Triton
Fountain

ST. ANNE STREET   FLORIANA, ST. PUBLIUS

In Freedom Square, you'll see the sad ruins of the classical old opera house built by E. M. Barry—a grim reminder of the bombing in World War II. To the right is Valletta's oldest church, the Baroque **Our Lady of Victories,** completed in 1567 to commemorate the Great Siege victory. (Its front was remodelled in the 17th century.) Next to it a crumbling reddish façade is what remains of one of the earliest houses built in the city. Opposite is the church of St. Catherine of Italy, a domed structure originally designed by Cassar, but later rebuilt.

A few steps further on, you come to the **Auberge de Castile et Léon,** most impressive of the *auberges**, now containing the office of the Prime Minister. It is a magnificent ochre stone construction originally built to Cassar's design, but rebuilt by a Maltese architect (Dominico Cachia) for the Portuguese Grand Master Pinto in the 18th century. Unfortunately the public can see this elegant structure from the outside only.

Just beyond Castile place are the **Upper Barracca Gardens,** built in the 18th century. With green shrubs and trees,

---

* The *auberges* (inns) are the buildings where the knights were accommodated. Each *langue* had its own *auberge.*

bright hibiscus and statues, the area is a pleasant retreat where the knights used to stroll and supposedly hatch plots, or where people watched the knights set off on expeditions. Among the statues you'll see today are a group of children, *Les Gavroches*, by Antonio Sciortino, the Maltese sculptor, a big monument to Lord Strickland, Prime Minister from 1927 to 1930, a bust of Sir Winston Churchill and the inconspicuous tomb of Sir Thomas Maitland, "King Tom", the intransigent governor from 1813 to 1824.

From under the colonnade here, there's a stunning **view**

The Prime Minister's office is housed in Auberge de Castille (left); sculpture is by Sciortino.

across the Grand Harbour. On the far left is the 17th-century Fort Ricasoli; directly ahead is Fort St. Angelo (an important stronghold in the Great Siege) at Vittoriosa; to the right, in Dockyard Creek, is where the knights had their boats repaired. Further along is Senglea (see p. 44), behind which rises the little town of Cospicua (because it's conspicuous, the guides tell you). To the right of Senglea, across the creek, a big dockyard project is under way. **33**

Finally, directly below, on Lascaris Wharf, is the old Customs House, attractively built in Venetian style.

Returning to Merchants Street, you'll see **Parisio Palace** on the right, where Napoleon stayed for a few days in 1798. Now the Ministry of Foreign Affairs, the palace is a sober 18th-century building. On the opposite side of the street, the Auberge d'Italie is an austere building built by Cassar in the 16th century and later modified. The mouldings at the corners ("quoins") are of interest.

Make your way from Merchants Street to **Republic Street** via Britannia Street. This main thoroughfare is a real beehive of activity, with all kinds of shops, cafés, snack bars and pharmacies. The **Church of Santa Barbara** (between South Street and Britannia Street) is unusual for its oval shape. This was the church used by the knights of the *langue* of Provence. The

decor is simple; the Roman Catholic services are held in English, French and German.

Conveniently near to the church, the **Auberge de Provence,** on the left going towards Fort St. Elmo, now houses the excellent **National Museum of Archaeology** (for opening hours, see p. 117). This *auberge*, founded in 1571 and designed by Gerolamo Cassar, is symmetrical, with Doric columns below, Ionic above, and interesting "quoins" on either side of the building. Its façade was remodelled in the 17th century. After the knights left in 1798, the *auberge* was lived in by several different groups of people and served for many years as the Union Club.

The museum collection, put together in the 17th and 18th centuries and reorganized by

Before age of bombers, Valletta's fortifications were impregnable.

Sir Themistocles Zammit, a famed Maltese scholar, was housed elsewhere until the inauguration of the museum in 1957.

It's essential to see this collection to better understand Malta's prehistoric sites. Some of the fascinating objects here are the famed small "Sleeping Woman" from the Hypogeum underground burial site, and the huge lower half of a "fat lady" transplanted from Tarxien, where she was getting eroded by the weather and elements. There are artifacts from all Malta's prehistoric periods, but some of the Tarxien ones are probably the most interesting—such as weapons and carbonized seeds, or a curious plate engraved with bulls and goats.

The shards of a few big bowls and vases from the Tarxien period have been reassembled. From the number found, it is thought that breaking vessels may have been part of the ancient religious cult.

Another exhibit, a case of skulls on the ground floor, shows the "long-heads" who were the first civilized Maltese settlers. These people disappeared completely later and were followed by settlers with differently shaped heads.

Upstairs, the museum

Of Palaces and Galleries

A large number of the palaces and noble buildings you'll see on Malta have rather blank, almost unfriendly façades. Privacy and security were of the utmost importance in the past and many buildings were entered only by an arched doorway on the side. Some palaces however have projecting and decorative stone balconies from the floor above the street level, with French doors opening onto them. In the inside of these palaces the plain architecture gives way to charming, sunny courtyards.

In Valletta, you'll also see many *galleriji* brightly painted wooden enclosed balconies. It was here that the strictly cloistered women of the past were able to get a glimpse of the outside world and, presumably, a breath of fresh air.

houses some interesting Roman and Punic (Carthaginian) items, especially two jewellery cases, and a *cippus* (small pillar) that has inscriptions in Phoenician and Greek on it, which enabled scholars to find the key for the deciphering of Phoenician. Its twin was given to Louis XIV and is now in the Louvre in Paris.

Several of the exhibits once on display at the National

Museum, including a collection of paintings, have been moved to the Fine Arts Museum in South Street (see p. 43).

After leaving the museum, if you turn down again towards Fort St. Elmo, you'll come to **St. John Square** and the Cathedral off to the right. The square contains a colourful outdoor market with carts and people filling it until noon. A crafts centre is housed in the square.

St. John's Co-Cathedral (for opening hours, see p. 117), the knights' own church, was built in 1577 to the plans of Gerolamo Cassar. It's considered to be his masterpiece and was raised to cathedral status in 1816 by Pope Pius VII. It's called "co-" because it shares the distinction with the earlier Mdina Cathedral.

Financed by funds contributed by Grand Master de la Cassière, who after the Great Siege was very keen to have all religious activity transferred from Birgu to Valletta as quickly as possible, the church has a rather heavy façade, which isn't likely to make you gasp with admiration. However, the interior reveals a staggering display of Baroque art. This elaborate production should be savoured at some length. Sir Walter Scott wrote that he had never seen a more striking church nave. The barrel-vaulted space is 189 feet long, 64 feet high and 115 feet wide. Everything in the enormous structure leads the eye up to the high altar. On both sides the nave is flanked with **chapels,** most of which were built by the various *langues* of the knights and named after saints. Every square inch of this church is carved in high relief with brightly painted religious motifs as sumptuous as a Rubens painting. Plenty of gilt touches add to the rich effect.

The polychrome marble paving on the floor covers the tombstones of the knights and is decorated with coats of arms, trophies, skeletons, and so on.

On the right-hand side of the nave, you'll see the chapels of St. James, St. George, St. Sebastian and the Blessed Sacrament. This last one has an extraordinary **screen** and **gates** in solid silver, which, legend says, were cleverly concealed by being painted black when the French were on a pillaging spree in their 1798 stay.

The vault of the church is decorated with oil-on-stone **paintings** by the 17th-century Calabrian painter Mattia Preti. The pictures tell the story of the life of St. John the Baptist, **37** and took the artist five years (1662–67) to complete.

The rich **high altar** (1681) was designed by architect Lorenzo Gafà, and presents an elaborate array of marble, silver-plate and lapis lazuli. The group behind the altar is of the Baptism of Christ, by Sicilian sculptor Giuseppe Mazzuoli.

The crypt, entered from the Chapel of Provence, may be visited on request between 10 a.m. and 12 noon; it contains the tombs of the first twelve Grand Masters.

Going back towards the entrance you'll see on the right the chapels of St. Charles (or of the Holy Relics), St. Michael,

St. Paul, St. Catherine and the Chapel of the Magi. Most chapels have busts or other monuments commemorating almost all the Grand Masters. In the sacristy there are paintings by Stefano Pieri, Preti and Antoine de Favray.

To reach the **oratory and museum,** take a door on the right facing the altar, third bay from the entrance. The oratory's main feature is the monumental painting by Caravaggio, *The Beheading of St. John*, widely esteemed to be the fin-

Horse-drawn karrozzin, *one way to see sights of historic Valletta.*

est painting in Malta. Commissioned by the Grand Master to paint several works, Caravaggio ended up by assaulting one of the knights. The details of the story are unclear but the artist left the country in disgrace in 1608. The painting is a rather lurid work, but dramatically moving, with good use of chiaroscuro and lively Baroque composition.

The museum contains the impressive Judocus de Vos **tapestries** which are hung out in the church nave in June. The 17th-century works are based on religious paintings by Rubens and Poussin.

Back on Republic Street and continuing towards Fort St. Elmo, you'll come to **Great Siege Square.** The square has a powerful allegorical monument by Sciortino. Opposite are the new Law Courts, a neo-classic colonnaded building, on the site of the Auberge d'Auvergne, bombed out in World War II.

Queen's Square, also off Republic Street, has a lifelike stone statue of Queen Victoria by the Sicilian sculptor Giuseppe Valenti. You'll also see a spacious outdoor café and little fast-food shops under the shady arcades.

At the back of the square is the **National Library.** Once the Library of the Order (and later the Royal Malta Library), it was constructed in the late 18th century mainly to house the large collection amassed by the knights.

A bit further beyond Queen Victoria's statue, you can go through a big arch into the first courtyard of the **Grand Master's Palace** (Magisterial Palace) and the Armoury. In 1569, the nephew of Grand Master del Monte built a large house here—probably the first private house in Valletta—and later the knights commissioned Gerolamo Cassar to enlarge the building into a palace. Today some parts house museums.

You'll find two cool, green courtyards in the palace grounds, one of them called Neptune Court, after its statue and the other, Prince Alfred's Court (the one nearest Queen's Square). Look out for the **clock** installed by Grand Master Pinto de Fonseca (1741–73), with little figures gonging the hours.

To visit the palace, take the staircase from Prince Alfred Courtyard. In the council chamber, formerly the meeting-place of Malta's Parliament, you can sit on one of the heavy bench-seats and admire the beautiful Gobelins **tapestries** given to the Order by

Grand Master Ramon Perellos in the early 18th century. Called *Les Tentures des Indes*, they represent all kinds of real and fanciful beasts and birds, with exotically clad Indians.

The grandest of the various public rooms is the **Hall of St. Michael and St. George,** or Throne Room, with a beamed ceiling and frieze by Matteo Perez d'Aleccio. Scenes of the Great Siege fill the walls, and the carved gallery comes from the ship in which Villiers de l'Isle Adam sailed away from Rhodes in 1523.

The damask-hung **Hall of Ambassadors** or Red Room features heavy and dark portraits of famous notables: Louis XIV by De Troy, Louis XV by Van Loo, Catherine II of Russia by Levitsky—a rather unfortunate rendering of that imposing monarch.

Other rooms to see include the State Dining Room, the Yellow State Room and the Prince of Wales Corridor.

The **Armoury,** at the back of the Palace, is notable for its immense collection of suits of mail; especially striking is the gold-inlaid **ceremonial suit** made for Grand Master Alof de Wignacourt, and some captured Turkish arms, including, it's said, the corsair Dragut's sword.

The Hospital of the Order
The splendid buildings and halls of the Mediterranean Conference Centre started as the hospital of the knights in 1574.

The knights took in anyone of any faith who was ill and treated the sick as *seigneurs malades* (sick lords) with respect and humility. The standard of medical treatment was high and the patients were given good food served on silver dishes. All the knights, from the youngest novices to the Grand Master, served the patients.

The hospital was taken over by the French when they occupied Malta and later by the British. During the war, the buildings were badly damaged by bombs.

Leaving the palace by the Neptune Court archway, you'll see the Greek Orthodox Church on Archbishop Street —unremarkable except for a 12th-century **icon** called Our Lady of Damascus, which the knights brought with them when they came to Malta in 1530. It was well restored in 1966.

Just a few steps away is the **Gesù Church,** built between 1592 and 1600, richly ornate in Italian Baroque style.

Take Merchants' Street down

to the **Mediterranean Conference Centre.** The restoration of
the badly bombed-out former
hospital of the Order is one
of independent Malta's finest
achievements. The feat was
accomplished in only a few
months, and the international
conference hall was opened in
1979.

The centre contains six well-
equipped conference rooms
as well as the beautiful 520-
foot-long hall that once served
as the Great Ward in the old
hospital. The largest of the conference halls is the Republic
Room, with a seating capacity
of over a thousand. For opening hours see p. 117.

*Shipwrecked St. Paul inspires a
cool, dark bar in Valletta street.*

Fort St. Elmo built in a star-
shaped design at the tip of
Valletta may be visited only
by special permission from the
government. However, within
the fort—that was so valiantly
defended, though finally lost,
in the Great Siege of 1565—
you can visit the War Museum
of World War II relics, including one of the three Gladiator
planes that constituted Malta's
air force when Italy declared
war in 1940, and General Ei-
senhower's jeep, "Husky". For
opening hours see p. 117.

Other Places of Interest

Proceeding back towards City Gate via Spur and Fountain streets, you'll come to Strait Street (also known as the Gut), a narrow, colourful and notorious lane which still has the bars and hangouts that have given it a reputation among sailors for low life. This street was the only place the knights were allowed to fight duels.

Close by is Independence Square, with a pretty view through to Marsamxett harbour. On the right you'll see the **Auberge d'Aragon,** the first *auberge* built in Valletta in the 16th century, with a Doric porch added later. Opposite, St. Paul's Anglican Cathedral was constructed in neo-classical style in the 19th century and paid for by the Dowager Queen Adelaide after a visit to Malta in 1838–39. Its 200-foot **bell tower** is a striking landmark.

The **Carmelite Church** on Old Theatre Street is another landmark. Its huge dome is 138 feet high. Severely bombed in the war, this larger church is still being rebuilt over the ruins of the old one.

The **Manoel Theatre,** built in 1731 under the rule of Grand Master Manoel de Vilhena, is a lovely 18th-century creation, one of Europe's oldest theatres still in use. At one time, the theatre underwent an unfortunate period of decay and became a cheap cinema, but it is now restored as Malta's National Theatre and is a gem, with its neat, oval shape, tiered balcony-boxes and delicate carving and painting. (Enter by Old Mint Street.)

There are several other Baroque churches to see in the old city, such as St. Roque and St. Ursula (both in St. Ursula Street) and **St. Paul Shipwrecked,** in St. Paul Street. This is a rich-looking 18th-century church with a 19th-century façade. Its outstanding treasure is a Baroque **statue of St. Paul,** carved by Melchiorre Gafà.

The **National Museum of Fine Arts** is on South Street, which crosses Republic Street up near City Gate. The building is an attractive white palace (16th century, later restored), built around a sunny courtyard, where contemporary exhibits are shown in the summer. Once used by the knights, it later served as the official residence of the Royal Navy's Commander-in-Chief.

The **collection** (most of which came from the National Museum of Archaeology) contains paintings from various periods of the Italian, Flemish and Dutch schools plus later **43** compositions by French artists Antoine de Favray, Claude Joseph Vernet and Louis de Cros. There are also some fine works of the 20th-century Maltese sculptor Antonio Sciortino.

The basement exhibit revives memories of the knights' hospital work, with vases, apothecary vessels and the famous elaborate **silverware** from which the knights served their patients.

Near City Gate (off to the right before you exit) are **Hastings Gardens,** named after the Marquess of Hastings, Governor of Malta from 1824 to 1826, whose funerary statue reposes in the gardens. From here there is a splendid **view** of Marsamxett Harbour—with Floriana, St. Publius Church and Independence Arena on the far left. You can also appreciate the huge **bastions** of St. Michael's and St. Andrew's here. They were built up after the Great Siege and are 60 to 70 feet thick. Across the way are Msida and Lazzaretto creeks, then Manoel Island, Dragut Point and Tigné Fort.

Walking back to City Gate before taking a staircase down, you'll cross the fortifications of St. James' Cavalier and St. John's Cavalier (the latter presently the knights' embassy in Malta).

Around Valletta

Floriana

Any approach to Valletta by land inevitably goes through the spacious Floriana area, named after Paolo Floriani, the Italian military engineer who recommended that Valletta be protected by outer fortresses on the land approach.

Here you'll drive under or beside the **Porte des Bombes,** a double arched gateway, one arch built in the 18th century, another built for aesthetic balance by the British. On St. Anne Street are the British and American embassies. St. Publius Church is a handsome two-towered building of the 18th century, named after Malta's first bishop. In an attractive garden setting nearby is the Phoenicia Hotel, the island's grandest old hostelry, a classic example of "British Colonial" style.

Vittoriosa, Senglea, Cospicua

Just on the other side of the Grand Harbour from Valletta are "the three cities", which you can reach by bus from City Gate, or after a pleasant, short ride in a *dgħajsa* (water taxi) from Customs House wharf (agree on a price in advance), or by car via Marsa.

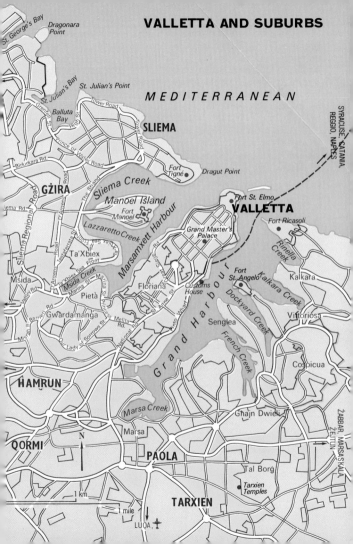

VALLETTA AND SUBURBS

St. George's Bay
Dragonara Point

St. Julian's Bay
St. Julian's Point

Balluta Bay
Grenfell St.

M E D I T E R R A N E A N

Tower Road

SLIEMA

Birkirkara Rd.

GŻIRA

Prince of Wales Road

The Strand

St. Agatha's Rd.

Sliema Creek

Fort Tigné

Dragut Point

SYRACUSE, CATANIA
REGGIO, NAPLES

Sliema Rd.

Manoel Island

Fort Manoel

Fort St. Elmo

VALLETTA

Fort Ricasoli

Sliema Regional Road

Lazzaretto Creek

Marsamxett Harbour

Grand Master's Palace

Rinella Creek

Ta'Xbiex

Ta'Xbiex Sea Front

Msida Creek

Customs House

Fort St. Angelo

Kalkara Creek

Kalkara

Msida

Pietà

Marina St.

Floriana

St. Anne St.

Dockyard Creek

Vittoriosa

Gwardamangia

Melita Rd.

Grand Harbour

Senglea

French Creek

Cospicua

Qt. Lady of Sorrows St.

National Rd.

HAMRUN

Marsa Creek

Għajn Dwieli

ŻABBAR, MARSASKALA
ŻEJTUN

QORMI

Marsa

PAOLA

N

Tal Borg

1 km

Tarxien Temples

1 mile

LUQA

TARXIEN

At the heart of **Vittoriosa,** in Majjistral (or Mistral) Street, is the pretty façade of the Auberge d'Angleterre. Nearby, the diminutive church on the lower left side of Vittoriosa Square is called St. Joseph's. You can ask for a key at the "museum" door around the corner—though there is not much to see inside except for a sword and hat belonging to Jean de la Valette.

Past a quiet square is the **Church of St. Lawrence,** originally the knights' Conventual Church before the move to Valletta. It was re-built by Romano Carapecchia in 1691 and is richly decorated inside

with paintings and pink marble columns. Outside, a plaque records the death of Sir Nicholas Upton, who fell defending Malta from the Turks in 1551. Another plaque commemorates the dead killed after bombing in World War II, when the church's dome was destroyed.

Below the church is a new Freedom Monument, unveiled on March 31, 1979, when the British Navy finally left for good: a British sailor shakes hands with a Maltese dockworker. The blue-painted buildings you'll see here were the Royal Navy's bakeries; now they are government property.

To visit **Fort St. Angelo,** you must apply to the Commandant for special permission (ask at the Tourist Office). It has an excellent view of the Grand Harbour, and was already built on in Phoenician times with, it is thought, a temple to Astarte, followed by a Greek temple to Hera and a Roman one to Juno. Within the fort, the Saint Anne chapel has a reputedly classical column. The fort was the Royal Navy's headquarters during World War II, and held up well, considering the number of times it was bombed.

Senglea and Cospicua were both heavily bombed in World War II, and have been re-built in rather uninspired modern style as suburban residential areas. SENGLEA, once called l'Isla, was named after the Grand Master who fortified it before the Great Siege, Claude

After the Great Siege, triumphant knights named town Vittoriosa. **47**

The Harbour by Boat

These conducted two-hour boat tours leaving from Sliema are excellent for a sea view of Valletta and environs. Various companies run the trips several times daily. A guide explains exactly what you're looking at, and you'll see things like the place where the knights put huge chains across the Grand Harbour to keep the Turks out, the wharves of the Grand Harbour Marina and big cruise-ships from Norway, Italy or Greece.

In one of the "creeks" are huge tankers, in another you'll see the dry dockyard project being built by the People's Republic of China; the looming 95-foot-high crane here is one of the world's largest, capable of lifting 150 tons. There are many more romantic vistas, however, including Valletta itself from the sea—a majestic group of fortresses, spires and domes.

de la Sengle. At Isola Point, it has a pretty little garden and a look-out post sculpted aptly with an eye and an ear. COSPICUA (also known as Bormla), is ringed by the formidable walls of the **Cotonera lines,** named after 17th-century Grand Master Cotoner.

Sliema and St. Julian's Bay

These are the lively high spots of Malta for hotels, nightlife and shopping.

Sliema, a thriving suburb of 24,000 people, is a lot larger than Valletta. It's about 3 miles from Floriana to Sliema's Strand, passing by or through the districts of PIETA, MSIDA and TA' XBIEX, none of them particularly pretty.

Sliema is quite new and has grown fast in recent years. Its general appearance might

best be described as undistinguished. Yet it has good shops, restaurants, hotels, and suitable flat spots along the rocky shoreline for swimming.

After St. Julian's Point with its fortified tower, now a pleasant café, you reach BALLUTTA BAY, and round the corner **St. Julian's Bay,** a quaint old fishing village that has several shops and a couple of good café-restaurants. Just a bit further along, before ST. GEORGE'S BAY, are some luxury hotels,

Dynamic tourist zone surrounds quiet village of St. Julian's Bay.

seaside discos and the Casino. The entire area swarms with bathers on summer weekends.

The huge St. Andrew's military base was a complete complex, with its own shops, banks and churches, but is now a bit of a ghost town; it's gradually being converted into residential and holiday flats.

49

Inland to Mdina and Rabat

Mdina is about 7 miles from Valletta, through busy, crowded HAMRUN, an industrial suburb. The road passes by the **aqueduct** built in the 17th century by Grand Master Wignacourt to bring water into Valletta.

Off to the right from ATTARD, you might want to take a detour to the **San Anton Gardens.** This is a refreshing, shady spot with exotic subtropical trees and flowers, some giant evergreens—possibly descendants of the islands' lusher days millenia ago when lots of rain and greenery brought abundant wildlife—and a mini-zoo. The President of Malta lives in the dignified, bougainvillea- and ivy-covered house at the opposite end of the gardens; it was built in the 17th century by Grand Master Antoine de Paule.

Further along the road, also branching off to the right, is TA 'QALI, a former airfield converted in 1972 into a crafts village (see p. 88).

Mdina

This historic citadel is one of Malta's most beautiful spots, a must for any visitor. The old city stands out like a splendid ship's prow at an altitude of 700 feet overlooking the plains and hills to the sea. It may have been inhabited since the Bronze Age, but in any case there were Punic and Roman settlements here. The Romans called it *Melita* (honey); St. Publius, the Roman governor converted by St. Paul and first bishop of Malta, lived here. When the Saracens fortified the promontory in the 9th century, they re-named it *Mdina* (the city) and separated it from its "suburb", Rabat.

Also known as Città Notabile, Mdina was the first capital of Malta, dating back to before Roman times. Later it was the Bishop's See and seat of the Università, the government advisory body. It was in Mdina that Roger the Norman was hailed as the island's liberator from the Arabs in 1090. When the knights decided that Valletta would be a better capital, Mdina became Città Vecchia (old city).

Now Mdina is known as "the silent city", intriguing and secretive within its narrow, nearly deserted streets. Its air of mystery is enhanced by the fact that several of Malta's aristocratic old families still live here—very discreetly in enclosed palaces.

To enter the city, there are

two large gates (both dated 1724) past the Howard Gardens and a bridged-over moat. The left gate is Greeks' Gate. Take the main **Mdina Gate** on the right. Just inside you'll see the harmonious courtyard and façade of a palace built in French style, **Vilhena Palace** (named after the Grand Master who had it built in the 18th century). It currently houses a quaint Museum of Natural History, whose most interesting exhibit is a three-dimensional display showing the geological "sandwich" of Malta and Gozo's rock formations. Across from the palace is the 16th-century Torre dello Standardo,

now the police station. **Villegaignon Street** is the town's main thoroughfare and runs straight through to the fortified edge of town.

To the right is the Convent of St. Benedict, a blank-walled building where no men are admitted. The two small churches are St. Peter's and St. Agatha's. On the left you'll see **Casa Inguanez,** the palace home of Malta's oldest titled family; the main entrance is around on Mesquita, a side street. The door is typical, with a good pair of brass Neptune knockers. Testaferrata Palace just off St. Paul's Square is an imposing building with a collection

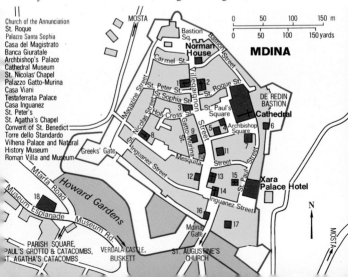

Church of the Annunciation
St. Roque
Palazzo Santa Sophia
Casa del Magistrato
Banca Giuratale
Archbishop's Palace
Cathedral Museum
St. Nicolas' Chapel
Palazzo Gatto-Murina
Casa Viani
Testaferrata Palace
Casa Inguanez
St. Peter's
St. Agatha's Chapel
Convent of St. Benedict
Torre dello Standardo
Vilhena Palace and Natural History Museum
Roman Villa and Museum

MOSTA

Bastion Sq.

Norman House

Carmel St.

Bastion Street

Villegaignon Street

MDINA

0   50   100   150 m
0   50   100   150 yards

Magazine Street

St. Peter St.

St. Sophia St.

St. Roque St.

St. Nicolas Street

Holy Cross Street

St. Paul's Square

Gatto-Murina Street

Archbishop Square

DE REDIN BASTION

Cathedral

Greeks' Gate

Inguanez Street

Mesquita

St. Paul Street

Street

Xara Palace Hotel

Maria Road

Howard Gardens

Museum Rd.

Museum Esplanade

Inguanez Street

Mdina Gate

N

MOSTA

PARISH SQUARE,
PAUL'S GROTTO & CATACOMBS,
ST. AGATHA'S CATACOMBS

VERDALA CASTLE,
BUSKETT

ST. AUGUSTINE'S CHURCH

of art but not open to the public.

The striking **cathedral** (seat of the bishopric and "co-cathedral" with St. John's in Valletta) is outstanding as a Baroque work on an island already abounding in Baroque art. Fronted by a pair of cannon, flanked by its two bell towers,

it has three doorways with two types of pilasters (Corinthian below, composite above), making an admirable façade when seen from the other end of the square.

The first church was built some time in the 13th century—according to legend, on the site of the house belonging to Publius. But all except the apse was destroyed by an earthquake in 1693. The new cathedral was built between 1697 and 1702 by Lorenzo Gafà and is considered his masterwork. The interior, under an impressive dome, is well-proportioned, yet very rich, especially the colourful floor—whose marble mosaic surface covers the tombs of bishops.

Noteworthy items to see in the cathedral: the heavy wooden **doors** through the vestry, carved with snakes and other motifs; a lively **fresco,** *The Shipwreck of St. Paul* by Mattia Preti, in the apse; to the left of the apse, a silver **processional cross,** brought to Malta (according to tradition) by the knights from Rhodes.

Just to the right of the Archbishop's Palace, outside the Cathedral, the former semina-ry now houses the **Cathedral Museum.** It contains much that was saved from the old cathedral, including exquisite 15th-century marquetry from the old choir, the bishop's carriage and various papal bulls. There are also Punic and Roman remains. The outstanding **coin collection** will thrill any numismatist and intrigue others; it is beautifully displayed in mirrored cases, to take you from Carthage all the way through to modern Europe, with a stop at many historical moments.

Upstairs is a collection of paintings from various schools (Sicilian, Flemish, Spanish, 16th–18th centuries), and an excellent group of Dürer woodcuts, plus engravings by Rembrandt, Piranesi, Van Dyck and Goya. And you might want to glance at a collection of beautiful illuminated choirbooks dating from the 11th century, as well as some valuable silver religious objects in another room.

Further along Villegaignon Street is the **Palazzo Santa Sophia,** reputedly the oldest house in Mdina, with a typical Maltese feature—a "stringcourse" of triangular corbels with balls attached to them.

The **Church of the Annunciation** is the next big building on the left; its bells played a

Mdina's cathedral boasts a Baroque façade worthy of the name.

part in the 1798 revolt. The French wanted to sell the valuable tapestries belonging to the church, but after an incident when a young boy attacked the French Commandant Masson, the bells were rung to call people from the neighbouring countryside. After a good deal of brawling, the enraged Maltese threw Commandant Masson to his death from the balcony of the notary's house. This was one of the first actions in the rebellion that would last until the French were ousted in 1800.

Near the end of Villegaignon Street on the right is the **Norman house,** or the Palazzo Falzon. The lower part was the earliest section of the house, a defensive façade with only slits for windows (14th-15th centuries). The later upper section has attractive double-arched windows.

At the end of the street, you'll come to a large bastion with a magnificent **view,** extending out to Mosta with its big red dome, all the way to the spires of Valletta in the east.

If you return to the cathedral via Bastion Street, to the left and parallel to Villegaignon Street, you might stop at a café for a drink and a sweeping view over south-east Malta.

Rabat

Before reaching Rabat, past Howard Gardens, you'll find the **Roman villa and museum** worth visiting. This small columned building in pinkish stone, garlanded by rhododendron, has been nicely restored. Inside, you can see remains from Greek, Carthaginian and Roman tombs. Downstairs in the atrium are some finely-drawn original mosaics. The technique is called "vermiculatum". The most amusing ones show two naiads beating up a satyr, and an elegant bird drinking out of a goblet.

Rabat itself is Mdina's suburb and contains both old and modern buildings. **St. Augustine's Church** on St. Augustine Street was built by Cassar, two years before Valletta's cathedral, and it foreshadows St. John's—especially the massive barrel-vaulted interior.

In the heart of Rabat on Parish Square is **St. Paul's Church** —a rich 16th-century building that some think was at least partly the work of Lorenzo Gafà, notably the big dome. The church at festival time (late June, early July) displays a particularly rich array of scarlet damask, 12-foot-high silver candlesticks and other valuables. The square outside, too, is exuberantly decorated.

In Rabat, islanders venerate St. Paul's Grotto, where the apostle is said to have sheltered for an entire winter in the 1st century A.D.

Just outside the church (on the left, downstairs) is **St. Paul's Grotto.** You can pay a few cents to have the cave lit where St. Paul supposedly sheltered when he was in Malta. Legend has it that no matter how much stone is extracted from the cave, by some miracle it always "grows" back.

The **catacombs** (St. Paul's and St. Agatha's; signs point there) are cool, maze-like galleries and passageways. The size suggests that a large Christian community lived in the area in the 4th and 5th centuries. The circular platforms are thought to be stone tables used for funeral feasts, and in some of the chambers prayers may have been held.

Verdala, Buskett, Dingli

Take the road from Rabat to Buskett, and **Verdala Castle** lies just east off the road, a few minutes from Rabat. You can visit only by special permission (apply to the Ministry of Works, The Palace, Valletta), but the view of it is striking. Once the summer residence of Grand Masters and Governors, it is now an official guest-house for important visitors. A square castle surrounded by a moat and pine groves, it was built by Gerolamo Cassar in 1586 as the summer residence of Grand Master de Verdalle, Cardinal Verdala. It has a magnificent **staircase** offering vast views.

The **Buskett** or Boschetto (meaning little wood) is Malta's most fertile green area, the spot where the knights raised their falcons for hunting. On June 28th and 29th, Malta's famed folklore festival is held here, and the quiet grove hums with singing and dancing.

The Inquisitor's summer palace, built in the 17th century, is a charming setting for such an awe-inspiring individual, who no doubt found the verdant surroundings a good place to relax from his weighty duties. Although recently restored, it is not open to visitors. Driving back via the south roads, you'll pass through a tiny village, DINGLI, and then over to the **Dingli Cliffs,** where you can enjoy a dizzying view of the sea from far above; over to the left is the tiny speck of Filfla island, made even smaller during and after World War II. (It was used by the British for bombing practice.)

South-East Coast

GĦAR LAPSI is a picturesque little village in a sheltered bay under the cliffs. Although the beach is small, the Maltese like to swim here. There are a few simple restaurants.

Further along, by the road that goes to ŻURRIEQ, is the **Blue Grotto**—not as large (or crowded) as the one in Capri, but some prefer this one. The approach road offers some spectacular views and leads to a small car-park, where you'll find a group of fishermen in their colourfully painted water taxis ready to shuttle you around the point and into the limestone caves. Try to go in the morning before 11, because this is when the light slants into the caves to reflect off the sheer white sand bottom. In some places your hand will literally glow a tasteful turquoise blue if you drag it in the water.

The 25-minute excursion takes in several caves, about which the fishermen give a little talk in English. The first cave is around 25 feet deep. It is tinted with lovely hues of pink, mauve and orange by coral and minerals in the limestone; you'll see the same effect in all three or four caves you visit, especially one called "Reflection Cave". The Blue Grotto itself could not be a more luminescent, pure blue, and coming out you'll see a square natural "window" in the rock, giving a fluorescent lamp effect.

Marsaxlokk on the eastern part of MARSAXLOKK BAY, is also known by the Italianized name Marsascirocco. It's Malta's largest fishing village, and with the calm blue water, bobbing *luzzu* boats, and the fishermen mending their red

Marsaxlokk housewife makes bags for souvenirs instead of fishnets.

nets, it's both colourful and genuinely peaceful. There are two similar baylets within the larger bay—St. George's Bay and Pretty Bay, which were once favourite haunts of well-off Maltese, though some industry and modern installations have made Pretty Bay less worthy of its name.

Dragut the pirate landed in Marsaxlokk in 1565 and in the 17th century several defensive towers were built, still in evidence. But this didn't put off Napoleon, whose troops disembarked here in 1798. A small road running down to Delimara Point takes you first past Tas-Silġ Chapel, where there is a Carmelite Monastery, and the site of a Punic-Roman temple considered to be dedicated to Astarte or Hera. Delimara Bay and Peter's Pool offer deep water rock swimming—a good way to escape beach crowds. At Xrobb il-Għaġin are some rather poor vestiges of a Neolithic temple.

About 3 miles from the temples, if you feel like walking, or a 15-minute drive around via Żejtun and Żabbar, is another smaller, charming fishing bay—**Marsaskala,** much like Marsaxlokk with its peaceful pastel houses. Both villages have at least one attractive and reasonable restaurant.

North-West Coast

The northern seaside coast of Malta stretches from St. George's Bay round the Marfa Ridge to Golden Bay. But first, also in the northern part of the island, about 3 miles inland, is the bustling little town of **Mosta,** worth visiting for its famed parish church alone, which is visible from all over the island.

The church, **St. Mary's,** was financed and built with local money and by voluntary labour between 1833 to 1860 to the design of architect Giorgio de Vassé, and the inhabitants are justly proud of it. The enormous **dome,** nearly 123 feet in diameter, was built without scaffolding, and is still one of the largest in the world. St. Mary's has a classical colonnaded façade, and the impression inside is one of "all dome", surrounded by apses. The geometrical marble floor heightens the dome effect. On the left side near the altar, a bomb fell through the dome on April 9, 1942, sliding across the floor without exploding—a miracle for those present.

Getting around in traditional style: donkey carts and fishing boats serve the purpose admirably.

Today you can view the bomb in the sacristy on the left; it's been defused.

Between Valletta and Mosta you pass through a group called "the three villages"—BALZAN, LIJA and ATTARD. These are pleasant if unremarkable residential towns with Baroque churches; nearby are the San Anton Gardens in Attard (see page 50).

Most of Malta's coastline north and west of Valletta slopes pleasantly to the sea, with plenty of rock bathing, and several good sand beaches. ST. GEORGE'S BAY, rather small, is pleasant for bathing, though somewhat crowded at times; it has cafés, facilities for all water sports and other amenities. Just north of it is the vast St. Andrew's base (see page 49).

After several points of land with their towers, you come to SALINA BAY, where on the right you'll see the John F. Kennedy Memorial Olive Grove, which has a small playground. The area is also a salt-pan and marshland. At QAWRA, further around, is a nice rock-sand place for bathing with a good restaurant and all water-sports facilities.

St. Paul's Bay is large and popular, with many small holi-
60 day houses dotting the shore-line, some sandy parts and lots of water sports. It is here that St. Paul supposedly stepped on to a nearby island after his shipwreck in A.D. 60. BUĠIBBA village turns into St. Paul's Bay town here, and a walk by the watchtower and around some of the little old houses is rewarding.

Just near the innermost curve of the bay at GĦAJN RASUL (which means "apostle's fountain") is the fountain said to be on the spot where St. Paul struck a rock which miraculously brought forth water. MISTRA BAY (a small bay within St. Paul's) is worth a short excursion. Following a road through Kalkara Ravine and a typical country landscape, you

Dominating the countryside for miles around, the dome of St. Mary's church in the town of Mosta is nearly as big as St. Peter's in Rome.

Landmarks on Mellieħa Ridge above splendid but crowded beach.

take a dirt road up to the redoubt which affords a grand **view;** the building was once a storage battery for the knights' artillery.

Mellieħa Bay, just under Marfa Ridge (which is the "tail" of fish-shaped Malta), is the most beautiful stretch of sandy beach on Malta, and it's very likely to be crowded on a fair Sunday.

Up the hill on Mellieħa Ridge, perched on a commanding spur, MELLIEĦA it-

self (a small town of 4,000 inhabitants) offers a superb **view** of Marfa Ridge, Comino and Gozo with its bell-towers in the distance. To the left of Marfa Ridge is the Red Tower, built by the knights in 1649. Halfway down to the beach, beyond the red and white oleanders, you'll see a spruced-up cave house, originally made as a bomb shelter in World War II.

Mellieħa's reddish stone 18th-century **church** stands proudly like a fortress on the promontory, though nestled in it is a chapel from the early Middle Ages, now a site of pilgrimage. Within the shrine is a small chapel with marble walls containing a **painting** of the Virgin said to be by St. Luke.

The northern shore of Marfa Ridge has several bays (some with sand) and swimming places, though the best-maintained is probably at **Ramla Bay,** with the modern hotel there. At ĊIRKEWWA is the landing place for the smaller, 20-minute ferry to Gozo.

The next bay is rocky but beautiful **Anchor Bay,** so named because it once had lots of large anchors on the shore. But you'll have to go back nearly to Mellieħa to drive there, as there is no road around the coast. The high cliffs on this side of Malta interrupt passage to the sea.

For the best accessible bays after Anchor Bay, Golden Bay and Għajn Tuffieħa Bay, take the road westward from St. Paul's Bay.

Golden Bay *(Ramla Tal-Mixquqa)* is edged with a golden crescent of sand, though it's not always pristine-clean. It is well-provided with hotels and cafés, and in the vicinity is a big new tourist complex, complete with swimming pool and outdoor dance floor. GĦAJN TUFFIEĦA BAY next-door is approached via a long staircase, and attracts fewer swimmers than Golden Bay.

The Prehistoric Sites

Malta's prehistory is impressive and enigmatic. It all began with a wave of agricultural immigrants who came over from Sicily between 5000 and 4000 B.C. Successive migrations followed and have now been classified into various periods and names that you'll encounter in looking at sites and visiting museums.

The different phases of Maltese prehistoric civilization are known as the Għar Dalam period, lasting up to about 4000 B.C.*; the Skorba phase, around 3600 B.C., characterized by its grey and red pottery; Żebbuġ (3200 B.C.); Mġarr (3000 B.C.) and Ġgantija (around 2800 B.C.). Outstanding in this latter period are the temples at Ġgantija on Gozo (see p. 77), Ħaġar Qim, an early temple at Tarxien and a temple at Mnajdra. The Hal Saflieni Hypogeum at Paola is a remarkable complex dating back to 2400 B.C. The Tarxien period (around 2200 B.C.) also left behind very impressive temples at Tarxien, Mnajdra, Skorba and Borġ in-Nadur.

Then came an unexplained

---

*All prehistoric dates given must be regarded as approximate.

Prehistoric Economics

How were the tombs and temples of ancient Malta produced and financed? This is a question that many archaeologists have asked themselves. The evidence suggests that the islanders lived peaceably together without trouble from outside neighbours. There was more rainfall thousands of years ago, so agriculture provided enough for the primitive people's needs.

A tribal system with tithes to the chief would have made it possible to achieve a structured society, able to pay priests and artisans, as well as providing sufficient funds to construct temples.

But the people must have imported flint and obsidian to be used as tools in their building, as these were not locally available. How they paid for these imports is still unsolved; though the medium of exchange may well have been something perishable, probably textiles and possibly even elaborate temple robes.

complete break (somewhere between 2400 and 2000 B.C.) in the temple-building civilization. Drought and starvation, emigration, religious hysteria and mass suicide are a few of the speculations put forward for the mysterious hiatus.

The next group of immigrants used Tarxien as a cemetery, and are called the Cemetery People. Finally, around 1400 B.C., came the Borġ in-Nadur (Bronze Age) period, with a settlement at Borġ in-Nadur. This was the last group of migrants until the Phoenicians in about 800 B.C.

Few hard facts are known about the type of religion practised by the temple-builders. Archaeologists have come up with a hypothetical cult related to both death and fertility. The presence of the huge, fat and skirted figure at Tarxien (the original is in the National Museum) would seem to suggest a fertility cult. A small terracotta "sleeping fat lady" (also in the National Museum) might be some sort of hope-prayer figure, or possibly a prophetess whose dreams had significance. There were also phallic symbols.

The construction of the temples was usually along the following lines. The curved outer walls were made of coralline limestone (a very hard limestone) with face or edge of blocks alternately projecting. Then came a packing of rubble and inner walls, usually of globigerina limestone. The final

At archaeological site at Tarxien, in the interior of Malta, a tourist snaps bas-relief carvings of mysterious sect's prehistoric temple.

roof-hole was covered with wood and/or brush. Doorways and passages were erected on the trilithon principle—which resembles post and lintel.

Most temples were built in series of lobes around a central court or passage; temples had three, four, five or six lobes or apses. Common features in-cluded sacrificial altars, possible "oracle chambers" and hollowed stones, perhaps for collecting sacrificial animal blood. Most temples were built behind a massive, concave entry wall.

Temple interiors and altars were decorated with carvings; and, though it seems hard to **65** believe, the carving must have been done with stone, since no metal tools have been found to correspond with this type of building. The great era of temple-building lasted from around 3500 to 2000 B.C.

During the Bronze Age, quite sophisticated metal-working techniques came to the islands, but the new race of immigrants produced nothing comparable to the earlier achievements. In roughly the same period of time, the Great Pyramid of Egypt (2575 B.C.), Stonehenge (2300 B.C.) and Knossós in Crete (2000 B.C.) were built. But the Maltese construction techniques are un-

related to these, and considered unique. It would seem the builders learned nothing from elsewhere, and invented everything themselves.

The following are some of the more interesting sites and caves to be visited. It is a good idea to go with a qualified guide if possible.

About 6 miles from Valletta, **Għar Dalam** is an important archaeological site. There is a small museum there, which shows the types of animals that existed on Malta in the Pleistocene era—such as hippopotamuses and dwarf elephants. At one time the sea covered Malta, then receded greatly, probably leaving a land bridge to Sicily, upon which the large animals made the crossing. As the climate grew drier, and food became scarcer, the number of animals gradually dwindled. Their bones and, later, human remains were found in the cave, a short walk downhill.

Uncovered from the late 19th century on, the natural cave intercepts a *wied*, or ravine, carved out of the hill by rushing torrents during the melting of an ice age. Caught in here were layers of detritus, including bones of wild animals. The human bones and carbonized grains found in the upper layers indicate that the cave was inhabited in Neolithic times and that the earliest settlers were an agricultural people. The cave is cool and restful, but there's not much to see except for stalactites and stalagmites.

Less than a mile away, on the way to St. George's Bay, is **Borġ in-Nadur,** a village that was fortified around 1500 B.C., with some remaining ruins and "cart-ruts" (see p. 14) nearby. Note the heavy wall fortifications.

Skorba at Żebbiegħ is the oldest dwelling site in Malta, with a wall built around 4000 B.C., remains of farmers' and herdsmens' huts and two megalithic temples.

Ħaġar Qim and Mnajdra can be reached via Żurrieq about 8 miles from Valletta. The site of **Ħaġar Qim** is spectacular—well above the sea, with a view onto Filfla island. Here you'll see a typical concave outer façade and a rather complex series of inside

Mystery pervades the Hypogeum, ancient cave-temple near Paola. Statue of "fat lady", opposite, may be clue to prehistoric fertility cult.

rooms. But the uniqueness of this temple lies in its construction material. It is almost wholly built of globigerina limestone, often pitted and weathered.

Interesting details here include various "mushroom" or "tea-table" altars in the second court as well as other altars with pit-hole decoration, a typical prehistoric Maltese temple decor. In the second "apse" on the right after entry, you'll see a small hole in a monolith and a space behind it, which may have been an oracle hole. One of Malta's famous "fat lady" figures was found in this temple. Known irreverently as "the Venus of Malta", the skirted cult-figure with piano legs but topless is now in the National Museum.

Mnajdra is a 5-minute walk down towards the sea on an even lovelier site. Contemporary with Ħaġar Qim, it is a complex of temples, with several features common to the former.

You reach the **Hal Saflieni Hypogeum** by going to Paola, a workers' suburb of Valletta. This eerie monument carved out of soft limestone is a vast, overwhelming, underground labyrinth, not recommended to sufferers from claustrophobia. Hypogeum is Greek for "under-ground". The caves were hollowed out in areas on three different levels, descending to a depth of 40 feet, and were discovered by accident when workers were building houses and digging cisterns here in 1902. Professionally explored by archaeologist Sir Themistocles Zammit, it's one of Malta's most fascinating prehistoric sites.

You descend a modern spiral staircase into the ever-danker and growing gloom. The first level would seem to be the oldest and roughest-cut (around 3000 B.C.). The two lower levels were made around the time of the Ġgantija and Tarxien Temples (2500–1800 B.C.) and were carved out with increasing care and sophistication. The middle level has curved-in walls, corbelling, doors and niches resembling the features of the above-ground temples. This can be best appreciated in areas called the Main Chamber and Holy of Holies. Another spooky room is called the Oracle Chamber, with a hollow where men (only, it seems) can make an odd echo effect. In the Main Chamber was found the "sleeping lady" statuette (now in the National Museum). Some rooms have decoration in red or black in the form of spirals or hexagons; one "wall drawing" is supposed to be of a bull. One of the niches off this level has a 6-foot-deep hole and is called, ominously, "the snake pit".

Down a narrow staircase to the deepest part, you'll notice cubicles and pits for what look like very watery graves. The whole complex covers an area of 8,600 square feet and is estimated to have contained some 6,000 or 7,000 bodies. Sheltered from the weather, this is undoubtedly ancient Malta's best-preserved monument.

In contrast to the troglodytical Hypogeum, very much in the sun and a garden setting, the **Tarxien temple ruins,** only 400 yards away, make a cheery change. The temples here were discovered by a farmer who had trouble ploughing up his field with all these megalithic stones in them; then Sir Themistocles Zammit enthusiastically jumped at the chance to uncover a new site, which was done from 1915 to 1919.

The three temples were built at different times, but the high period dates from about 2400–1800 B.C.—the ultimate flowering of temple-building. First you'll see a museum with replicas of interesting carved stones found here, plus another piano-legged "fat lady". Then the first temple you come to contains replicas of lively bas-relief carvings—spirals, sheep, goats, pigs, cattle. Here you'll see yet another replica of a "fat lady", whose generous proportions will be an inspiration to weight-watchers.

The second temple is original in having six lobes or oval bays off the main corridor, instead of the usual four or five. Here you'll see a circular hearth, where the walls are rust-coloured from an ancient fire, possibly the result of the cremations. To the right is a small room containing slabs with interesting original carvings—bulls and a sow suckling her litter. Part of the floor has been removed to show the heavy stone balls that were used as rollers for the monolithic slabs.

The third temple of the group is the oldest including, a little further on, fragmented remains of the ancient Ġgantija-period temple. Beyond this, on the way out, you'll see a geometrically arranged series of round hollows in a big slab; this could have been a game, or used for divining purposes, though it's considered more likely that the depressions had to do with primitive libation ceremonies.

Gozo

Called Calypso's Island, because the famed siren supposedly kept Ulysses enthralled there for seven blissful years, Gozo is still enchanting to people who like its sleepy pace and rustic whimsical charms. To the Maltese, it's known as Għawdex (pronounced "owdesh").

Gozo is Malta's small sister, only 9 miles long by 4½ miles wide, with a population of almost 30,000. And while its history and development parallel Malta's, Gozo has its own distinct characteristics. The natives, called Gozitans, are proud of their island.

Gozo is greener than Malta. The scenery is characterized by neat terraces and freestone fences, with big flat-topped mesas rising on the horizon, and bell-towers silhouetted against the sky of every town. The island is church-mad, and there are at least 29 parish churches, not to mention little chapels. A day in any town is punctuated throughout by church bells ringing their various messages.

While 20th-century traffic has taken over the small roads, life still goes on much as it did centuries ago. Gozo lives mainly on agriculture and fishing, with excellent crops of tomatoes, potatoes, melons, oranges and figs. People are close to the earth, and you'll still see farmers leading their flocks of goats or driving donkey carts, while little old ladies make lace in the shade of their doorways in the late afternoon.

Activity centres around the hub and capital city of Victoria, although there is much to see elsewhere. Many people try to cram Gozo into one day, but this is a shame, since the small island should be savoured at leisure. It not only has numerous interesting Baroque churches, but the spectacular Neolithic temples of Ġgantija, plus fascinating hikes and rough swimming. (Beach life can be beautiful here, but it's also primitive, and you won't find a sophisticated cabana setting.) There is only one luxury hotel, but the small simple hotels and restaurants can be very pleasant. So pleasant that a number of Britons have chosen Gozo as their retirement home.

There is no airstrip on the island, so you go from Malta by ferry, private boat, or an excursion day tour from Sliema. Whichever route you take, from Sa Maison near Valletta or from Ċirkewwa, the short crossing is delightful. On the right, you'll pass uninhabited Cominetto rock and Comino with its watchtower, though you won't see the island's one hotel, in a bay on the other side. The name Comino comes from the herb cumin, which was once grown in abundance there.

The entry into Mġarr harbour is exciting, with several beautiful belfries looming up on the hills, the harbour itself alive with bobbing *luzzu* boats. On the left the tall steeple belongs to a 19th-century church, Our Lady of Lourdes. On the headland is Fort Chambray, built in the mid-18th century by a French knight. Later it became the prison, but since there wasn't much crime on Gozo, the prison closed (miscreants are sent to Malta) and the building is now used as the island's mental hospital.

The ups and downs of Gozo's history are very similar to those of Malta's. From the prehistoric temples of Ġgantija, which have much in common with the Tarxien temples, to the aggression of the Turks, then British rule and finally independence, the story of Gozo reflects that of Malta.

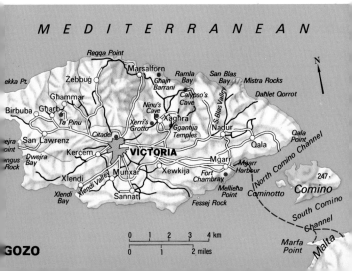

MEDITERRANEAN

N

Reqqa Point
Marsalforn
Ramla Bay
San Blas Bay
Mistra Rocks
ekka Pt.
Żebbuġ
Għajn Barrani
Daħlet Qorrot
Ghammar
Ninu's Cave
Calypso's Cave
S. Blas Valley
Birbuba
Għarb
Xerri's Grotto
Xagħra
Ta' Pinu
Citadel
Ġgantija Temples
Nadur
Qala Point
ejra
San Lawrenz
Kerċem
VICTORIA
Qala
ngus oint
Dwejra Bay
Rock
Mġarr
Mġarr Harbour
North Comino Channel
247.
Xlendi
Munxar
Xewkija
Fort Chambray
Comino
Xlendi Bay
Xlendi Valley
Sannat
Mellieħa Point
Cominotto
South Comino
Fessej Rock
Channel

0   1   2   3   4 km
0   1   2 miles

Marfa Point

Malta

GOZO

Victoria

The English doggedly call Gozo's bustling centre by the name given it during Queen Victoria's jubilee in 1897, though Gozitans call it by its old Arab name, Rabat. Just a short drive (about 3½ miles) from MĠARR, the town has a citadel situated on a bluff, which can be seen for miles.

The main street is **Republic Street** (Racecourse Street). On the left, Rundle Gardens are named after Sir Leslie Rundle, governor of Malta, 1909–15. During the August 15 Feast of the Assumption, this is the site of a charming little country

fair. During the same period (and also on the Feast of St. George, third Sunday in July) a colourful horse and donkey race is run, when everybody turns out to see their friends race in sulkies or ride the mules bareback up Republic Street— quite a hilarious occasion.

It-Tokk is the attractive shady central square, with a war monument in the middle,

Spires of Our Lady of Lourdes church dominate Mġarr harbour, Gozo's gateway. Handmade pullovers (left) take hours of patient work.

edged with little shops, tiny tunnel-shaped bars and a bank. On one side is the 18th-century St. James' Church, on the other a rounded building that was built in 1733 to house the Banca Giuratala; today it is the tourist office, though many local worthies seem to use the place as a haven for reading their newspapers.

During *festa* times, the square is a riot of colour with various religious statues; "Judas" is appropriately placed just outside the Inland Revenue Office, and there are garlands all over the square. But any morning it is a hub of seething activity with an open-air market. In the evenings, it swarms again, with people walking slowly up and down for the *passeggiata* or social hour.

Market times are good for exploring the back streets, when you'll see a lavish display of fish, fruit and vegetables, and hear lively banter between shoppers and sellers. The **old town** behind It-Tokk is very picturesque, with narrow alleyways and simple old houses.

On its own square, **St. George's Church** is a fine example of Baroque architecture, and very elaborately decorated. Though restored in the 19th and 20th centuries (with a whole new Romanesque-style roof), the original church was built much earlier, then improved and enlarged after 1673 when the Gozitans contributed their wealth and services in thanksgiving for having escaped a plague that raged that year. The most striking **painting** is by Mattia Preti over the choir altar, showing St. George with his foot victoriously poised on the dragon's head, his white charger by his side. The July festival is quite a bash, and there is a good deal of rivalry between St. George's and the cathedral, whose festival is the Assumption, August 15.

The citadel contains the **cathedral.** It is possible to drive from It-Tokk all the way up to the building, where there is a small parking space. Behind the rather austere stone façade with its two huge bronze cannons at the entry is an elaborate interior. Built by Lorenzo Gafà between 1697 and 1711, it has an interesting and convincing *trompe l'œil* "dome" painted on a flat space by Antonio Manuele; the real dome was never finished. Be sure not to miss the coloured mosaic tombs of bishops and priests, with their family crests and Latin mottoes on the floor.

On the left as you enter is a

rather histrionic statue of the Virgin, all in blue, her eyes and hands raised heavenward; this 20th-century work is carried all around town during the festival of the Assumption, and is posed on a very ornate and expensive-looking heavy silver pedestal.

Outside through a little gate to the left of the cathedral is the Bondi Palace, now containing the **Gozo Museum**. The house, built around an inner courtyard, was once owned by a distinguished local family. Among the exhibits are amphorae from Roman times, a 12th-century tombstone of an Arab girl with a touching inscription, and shards and relics from various eras, especially the prehistoric phases. It has a model of Ġgantija as well as a large phallic symbol from one of Ġgantija's temples. A visit will provide a good introduction to the temples you can see at Xagħra (see p. 79). Upstairs is a handsome headless female

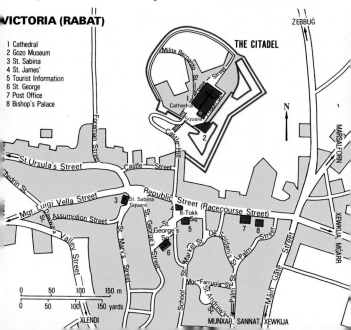

VICTORIA (RABAT)

ŻEBBUĠ

THE CITADEL

1 Cathedral
2 Gozo Museum
3 St. Sabina
4 St. James'
5 Tourist Information
6 St. George
7 Post Office
8 Bishop's Palace

Milite Bernardo St.

Cathedral Square

Castle St.

N

MARSALFORN

XEWKIJA, MĠARR

St. Ursula's Street

Castle Street

Foreman Street

hedrin St.

Mgr. Luigi Vella Street

Assumption Street

Republic Street (Racecourse Street)

St. Sabina Square

It-Tokk Sq.

St. George's Sq.

De Soldan's St.

Palm St.

Main Gate St.

XEWKIJA, MĠARR

Valley Street

St. Mary's Street

St. George's Street

School St.

St. Market St.

St. Andrew's St.

Mgr. Farrugia St.

MUNXAR, SANNAT, XEWKIJA

0   50   100   150 m
0   50   100   150 yards

XLENDI

Roman statue, dated to the 1st century B.C.

Climb the steps on the other side of the cathedral courtyard and you'll reach the ramparts of the citadel. In a 20-minute walk around, you can admire marvellous **views** all over Gozo, with its flat-topped houses edging the meandering roads and a church on nearly every hilltop. The citadel and ramparts were strengthened after the brutal Turkish incursion and kidnappings of 1551. Dragut, the North-African pirate (see p. 19), having failed in an assault against the knights in Malta, attacked the people of Gozo, carrying off between 6,000 and 7,000 islanders to slavery. Subsequently, Gozo was invaded many times by the Turks in the 16th century and gradually the stone dwellings of the citadel were abandoned. Though the rubble where goats graze looks as deserted as Ġgantija, it is earmarked for restoration with the assistance of UNESCO.

Ġgantija Temples

To reach this ancient site, you take the road to Xagħra, but before entering town, on the right, there's a fenced enclosure. Here you'll find the most awe-inspiring of any temple group in the Maltese islands.

The Ġgantija temples were excavated at various times between 1827 and 1953. There are two of them, both facing south-east as most prehistoric temples in Malta do.

The oldest and biggest of the temples dates back to around 2800 B.C., a period sometimes referred to as the Copper Age (precursor to the Bronze Age), though there was no copper on Malta or Gozo then. Typical of this type of temple, the façade is slightly concave. The entry is flanked by two orthostats (upright stones), a big slab, and a concave stone where worshippers may have washed their feet. The left part of the façade is made of huge coralline limestone slabs, rising to a height of about 20 feet. Here you can really appreciate the name—Ġgantija—and legend says that a monstrous woman or a group of colossal giants built the temples.

The inside walls and decoration are of softer globigerina limestone. The lobe-shaped apses (five of them) contain a number of interesting features, including libation holes, an oracle hole (on the right) and stones carved with typical swirling patterns. In the second right-hand apse, you'll see a fireplace hole, probably used to keep an "eternal flame" burning.

One of the blocks on view **77**

Time off at a bar on Gozo; the wine has an ample alcohol content.

once supported the huge phallic symbol in the Gozo Museum. Two nearby apses and the rear apse constitute the "holy of holies", and were probably restricted to priests. This apse has impressively high walls—20 feet or so—and is curved inward, to make a semidome. The altar, with two holes, perhaps for draining animal blood, has three blocks with primitive pitting decorations, typical of the period.

The smaller temple is simpler and rather less interesting, with the rear or main apse and altar reduced to almost nothing. A walk outside around the walls shows the skill of these early builders, who used enormous blocks of hard coralline limestone, placed horizontally and vertically, some of them 16 feet long and weighing up to 50 tons. The technical feat performed by primitive men, who supposedly knew no mathematics, in erecting these blocks boggles the mind. It was hypothetically done by a system of levers and ramps, using both gravity and manpower in the manœuvring process. An excellent little booklet you can buy gives all the fine details.

Towns and Villages

North-west of Ġgantija, **Xagħra** was inhabited in prehistoric times. It's a pleasant town with an exuberantly decorated red "Baroque" 19th-century **church.** Signs point to Xerri's Cave and Ninu's Cave, and both are worth a short visit. Guides will point out the amusing shapes of the stalactites and stalagmites.

At the north-east corner of the Xagħra plateau, with a superb view over to Ramla Bay on the right, you come to **Calypso's Cave**, where Ulysses supposedly dallied with the siren. One wonders what either Calypso or Ulysses saw in this place, as the narrow staircase leads to a singularly unimpressive and murky hole.

Almost directly across the central road to Mġarr, is **Xewkija,** a rather plain town with an awesome **church,** started in 1952 and still having the finishing touches put on. Built to a classical design in golden globigerina limestone, it is a typical Gozitan accomplishment, realized by the labour and devotion of the town's 3,500 citizens. The **dome** here is even bigger than Malta's Mosta, and the third or fourth largest in the world. (Internal diameter 80 ft., height 245 ft.). The parishioners wanted the church so badly, they built it right over the old one, only removing the first when the new building could be used.

Xlendi is reached by a small road leading south-west out of Victoria. Two miles from the island capital, it is a lovely natural site worth the trip, though it can be crowded. On the way, you'll see hilly pastoral scenery, a monumental wash-house on the left adorned with the arms of the Order, and, at a turning on the right, the slaughter-house. Xlendi is beautifully situated at the end of a long *wied* (a natural fissure in the rock caused by erosion).

The pastel houses of the town are tucked away at the end of a long narrow bay surrounded by two high rocky promontories. (Along the left-hand promontory is a favourite place for swimming, and the right-hand one is a nice place for hardy walkers.) With a small hotel and a couple of modest cafés and restaurants, Xlendi is a favourite excursion haunt. Tourists love the little shops where lace, woven goods and other local specialities are sold.

An adjacent road out of Victoria leads to **Sannat,** a tiny town reputed for its lace-making. Just outside is the island's only luxury hotel, Ta'Ċenċ, built in native stone and discreetly hidden in the countryside. It's near a huge new reservoir that is a boon to the neighbouring towns. Ta'Ċenċ is also in the vicinity of a site full of prehistoric "cart tracks" (see p. 14).

All roads lead from Victoria, and Marsalforn is about 2½ miles to the north-east. On the way, you'll see several windmills and, to the left, a statue of Christ crowning a peak.

Once a quiet old fishing town, **Marsalforn** has become a popular bathing place, especially the over-crowded spit of sand next to a modern hotel, and the rock ledges. Off to the left, a small road leads to the Nun's Pool, where Franciscan nuns bathe in their modest knee-length costumes in the late afternoon, and farther along to a beautiful stretch of salt-pans.

From Marsalforn, a road leads through some rugged country a couple of miles up to ŻEBBUĠ, which has little of merit except good views. (You can also take a larger road from Victoria.) There is a quaint informal exhibit here which a local family will be glad to show you. Ask anybody for the house of Sebastian Axiak, a local farmer who turned his hand to sculpting and made a big **diorama;** he died years ago, but the family is happy to display the diorama, a charming potpourri of Christian lore, village scenes and bell-towers from all over the world.

West of Victoria is Gozo's most primitive and, some think, prettiest area. Latest of all places to have been settled, it was once called "the desert".

On a side road between GĦAMMAR and Għarb is a curious church, **Ta'Pinu,** built between 1920 and 1936. This incongruous neo-Romanesque affair is surrounded by oleanders and a circle of large white statues depicting the Stations of the Cross, but its main interest lies in the miracles connected with it. This was the site of a rather run-down chapel (1534), which had been cared for by a pious man named Gauci, nicknamed Pinu. On June 22, 1883, a peasant woman named Carmela Grima heard a mysterious voice urging her to say three *aves.* She heard a similar voice several times, and a friend of hers, Francesco Portelli, admitted he had heard voices too. The two prayed for his desperately ill mother, who recovered miraculously, and from then on miracles multiplied. Ta'Pinu is still a famous shrine and place of pilgrimage, with a flock of votive objects left in the church.

Nearby, just outside Gharb, the museum is a quaint little place with small objects and dioramas made by the pious Portelli and Carmela Grima. To see the museum, ask the parish priest at Ta'Pinu, who can arrange to have it opened.

Gharb is the perfect little

Sitting, standing or sunbathing, the sunshine makes everybody equal at the delightful fishing hamlet of Xlendi, two miles south-west of Victoria.

Resolute farmer scrapes a living from cactus-barbed Gozo terraces.

Gozitan village boasting a lovely Baroque church on its main square. With pastel house-fronts, a tiny village shop and little to do except watch the women making lace, the scene is so peaceful that it almost seems unreal. The square is beautifully decorated with coloured pillars and lights at *festa* time in early July.

Back towards Victoria, take

a small road outside Gḣarb through SAN LAWRENZ, then left about a mile down to **Dwejra** for some spectacular sightseeing and bathing. Across the cliffs as you descend is a big outcrop in the water—Fungus Rock, so named for a fungus growing there which was once prized by the knights for its curative haemostatic powers. The bay below is dominated by Qawra Tower, built in 1651. Just beyond, a little chapel to the left is on an extraordinary rock promontory with a natural opening. Down a rocky road to the right is the **Inland Sea,** a quiet salt-water pool with a scenic tunnel through which you can swim (about 10–15 minutes) or ride in a fisherman's boat out to the open sea. There are no amenities here, but a friendly fisherman's hut opens up as a "bar" in the summer.

Nadur, 3½ miles east of Victoria, is the second largest town in Gozo, population 4,300, and the richest. The people are proud of their parish **church,** built by G. Bonnici in the 18th century, restored in the 19th, and rich in elaborate and expensive decor. The town is at quite an altitude for Gozo—500 feet above sea-level—and the name Nadur means "summit" in Arabic.

For isolated rock bathing in a very pretty and spectacular setting, you can take a little rutty road north of Nadur, then walk down past the orange groves to **San Blas.** Another road leads 2 miles to **Ramla Bay,** where you'll find Gozo's big golden-sand beach. It has a simple bar in summer, and plenty of sunning space despite its popularity. North of Ramla is GĦAJN BARRANI, accessible only by a primitive road which stops at the head of a cliff that you have to scramble down; but the setting is lovely, and the rocks are flat—for sunbathing or picnics.

QALA is a simple country town whose windmill is the last one working in Gozo. Further on are coves with good bathing, and quarries whose main claim to fame is that they supplied the white stone for the new Roman Catholic Cathedral of Liverpool.

As in Malta, almost everything is an excursion on Gozo. If you're staying there, a pleasant half-day's outing can be made by hiring a boat for a trip around GOZO and COMINO. There are lovely rocky outcrops and headlands, and you can stop in the popular blue lagoon for a refreshing swim in limpid turquoise water. **83**

What to Do

Sports

With its beneficent climate, Malta is a paradise for all outdoor sports most of the year. About the only things you can't do here are ski and ice skate. Naturally, water sports come first on the islands, but hiking around the rocky headlands and to archaeological sites can be a wonderful—and free—occupation in the cooler months.

Swimming

It's free everywhere except for a few spots where you can rent a mat or chaise-longue for a reasonable price and enjoy the benefits of a bar or restaurant. There is plenty of sandy beach room on Malta, less on Gozo. Best bets in Malta are Golden Bay, Għajn Tuffieħa, Gnejna Bay, Paradise Bay and Mellieħa Bay. On Gozo, the big sandy crescent is Ramla Bay. San Blas Bay is smaller and less accessible.

But even prettier scenery and snorkelling can be enjoyed at the rocky beach sites (and you won't get sand in your sandwiches). Some of these are Peter's Pool and Għar Lapsi

Pool; St. Paul's Bay; Marsaskala. Sliema offers flat rocks for sunbathing, but sometimes the area is crowded. Gozo's attractive rock-bathing beaches include Xlendi (sand as well), the Inland Sea (Dwejra), Marsalforn, Mġarr ix-Xini, Daħlet Qorrot, and Qala (near the desalination plant).

Unconcerned by nautical traffic, scuba diver prepares for plunge.

Water Skiing

The larger beaches and big hotels offer most water sports and facilities. There's water skiing at St. Paul's Bay, Mellieħa, Sliema, Salina Bay, St. George's Bay, Golden Bay.

Scuba Diving and Snorkelling

Snorkelling is good everywhere you swim, and is a sport you can do with minimal instruction. Masks and breathing equipment may be bought, or you can rent everything at beach centres, including flippers and safety floats.

Scuba diving and instruction are available at St. Julian's, St. Paul's Bay and Mellieħa Bay. You must hold a diving permit, available from local health authorities. The scuba diving centres will give you full instruction. You can also go on diving day trips to Gozo and Comino.

Underwater fishing is prohibited to protect marine life.

Boating and Sailing

As a top Mediterranean seaport, Malta naturally has excellent facilities, and if you don't come in your own boat, you can rent anything from a luxury craft right down to a simple dinghy. Information on berthing, repairs, and firms chartering boats is available from Malta Yachting Centre, Manoel Island Bridge, Gżira. See p. 104 for rental charges. The Valletta Yacht Club on Manoel Island accepts temporary members.

Fishing

It's free and you don't need a licence. If you want to go out early with a fisherman, inquire informally around Marsaxlokk Bay or in Mġarr harbour on Gozo. A fisherman might take you out for a small fee or even for nothing.

Sea swimming and sailing are two of many outdoor sports in Malta.

The Marsa Sports Club

This sports centre is the main place to offer many inland sports, including golf, tennis, squash, riding, cricket—and billiards. It is $2^1/_2$ miles south of Valletta at Marsa, on the way to Luqa Airport, and has a modern, fully-equipped club house with a bar and restaurant. The club has over a dozen hard tennis courts, an 18-hole golf-course and a squash court. Riding, polo and horse-racing can also be found at Marsa.

Spectator Sports

The Maltese are mad about **football** (soccer). Main matches of the Football Association take place at the Stadium, Gżira, from October to June. A new sports stadium is under construction at Ta'Qali (Mdina).

Water-polo is played all over the island, under the aegis of the Amateur Swimming Association. Inquire at the Tourist Organization.

Other Sports

There is a big bowling centre at Msida (Enrico Mizzi Street), open daily from 10 a.m. to 1 a.m. Archery, table tennis and badminton are also available through the Marsa Sports Club.

Shopping

There is only one big department store (in Floriana), so you'll usually make your purchases in small specialized shops or buy from outdoor stalls. Prices are reasonable on the whole, and the figure shown or quoted is the real price; haggling is not a way of life here. For shopping hours, see HOURS, p. 117.

Best Buys

Malta and Gozo are a bonanza if you're in the market for silver, glass, ceramics, cotton goods, sturdy woollen knits, woven gloves and lace. Ta'Qali just outside Mdina, is a recently developed crafts village that welcomes visitors (see p. 50). Here, in "quonset huts" on a converted airstrip, you can see artisans at work and buy their wares inexpensively. The glass factory offers lovely shapes and marbled colours in hand-blown Mdina glass. The subtle blend of turquoise blue and bottle green is outstanding, as is another combination of browns. This unique look was started by two Englishmen and enthusiastically adopted by the Maltese. You'll see everything here from vaguely triangular decorative fish to goblets and "Ming" jars.

The silver and filigree shown at Ta'Qali is interesting, including many Maltese crosses, rings, bracelets of varied design, cigarette boxes and candelabra.

The pottery and ceramics are rather rustic but of high quality, including brown and blue fired vases, ash trays, dishes of all sizes, and other objects that could not fail to look pretty in a country setting. A workshop also sells "Malta Stone", a type of banded calcite worked into bookends, ash trays and so on.

There is also a crafts centre opposite the cathedral in St. John's Square, Valletta, and other shops selling the same type of goods described above, especially dazzling silver. Maltese silver is reputed to have the highest pure silver content in the world. Gold can also be a good buy in Malta—small objects and jewellery.

Weaving, knitting and lace-making are still flourishing on Gozo (sometimes sold on Malta), and Gozo's main good buys are lace and woollen knits. The lace can be very delicate, on handkerchiefs, all-lace doilies, or as edging for place-

Life in the Mediterranean is lived outdoors, even the shopping—for seafood or clothing or souvenirs.

88

mats, napkins and tablecloths, attractive in oatmeal-coloured linen. Triangular loosely knit shawls are inexpensive and useful for cool evenings. And you might want to take home a Gozo sweater—either a practical, nautical-looking pullover or a belted cardigan with a shawl collar, usually in white or off-white, sometimes in subtle colours as well. The wool varies from very soft, almost angora quality to rather prickly. Sizes are the same for both women and men. Best places to shop on Gozo are around Victoria's It-Tokk square, in Xlendi and Marsalforn.

Other good buys on both Malta and Gozo include inexpensive cotton goods: bikini bathing costumes, nice dish towels, funny bikini underwear for women, attractive T-shirts for women and men, and jeans (Gozo makes them).

Naturally, you'll find plenty of colourful postcards and the run-of-the-mill "scene" souvenirs—ash trays, flags and so on with *luzzu* or *dghajsa* boats, knights' fortifications and watchtowers, the Maltese Cross and knights' coats of arms all over the place. Wrought ironware is becoming an interesting local buy, and traditional brass dolphin door-knockers make good souvenirs.

90

Festivals

The Maltese are a very festive people, celebrating anything at the drop of a hat; luckily there are dozens of religious holidays throughout the year. Unique to the Maltese islands are the saint days, celebrated as joyous *festi*. Every parish (64 in Malta and 14 in Gozo) celebrates its patron saint day, though dates vary and are usually on the weekend after the day itself.

Most **festi** happen throughout the summer, beginning with three days of prayer services preceding the eve of the celebration. Thanksgiving mas-

National Tourist Organization - Malta

ses are said in the mornings, and the churches are decorated with flowers, huge silver candlesticks, and sometimes red silk damask hangings. Outside, the façades are lit by garlands of light. On the eve of the feast-day the main religious service is marked by the removal of the holy relic from the side chapel to the altar. On the day itself, brass bands parade around town, while groups of men carry a statue of the saint, and the joyous crowd has a ball with fireworks and ice-cream cones. There is a concert in the town's main square, followed by an often excellent fireworks display, usually on Saturday night. The Tourist Office can usually supply you with the dates of the year's *festi*.

Christmas and Easter are celebrated solemnly but also with good food (the *figolla* is a traditional Easter sweet), gaiety and goodwill. Good Friday is marked by processions with marching, hooded *penitentes* carrying statues in the streets, as in Spain or South America.

Fanciful costumes, dancing and merriment enliven Maltese carnival; some traditions stem from celebration of victory in 1565 siege.

National Day falls on March 31. It is celebrated at Valletta and Vittoriosa with parades, marching bands, fireworks and sporting events.

Carnival is quite a lively occasion in Malta, held in mid-May (second weekend). Though "carnival" is an ancient celebration, the knights started the Maltese version. The celebrations begin with the dancing of the *parata*, a sword dance, to commemorate the knights' victory over the Turks in the siege of 1565. The high point of carnival was in the 18th century, when the knights paraded in grand carriages, to the accompaniment of drums and fireworks. Though not as elaborate today, there are still decorated floats and cars led by King Carnival, and folk-dancing contests.

The **Imnarja** is a folk festival held on the weekend preceding June 29 in the evening in Buskett Gardens, with lots of music, singing and dancing, plus horse races and donkey races nearby.

The **Regatta** or the Commemoration of the Two Sieges (1565 and 1940–43) is a joyous occasion on the Sunday following September 8.

Republic Day on December 13 is celebrated in Valetta with parades, music and fireworks.

Nightlife

Malta may lack the sophistication of the world's fleshpots, but there's plenty of activity after dark, from the cocktail hour on (though not very late). Even lively Sliema is rather restful after midnight.

Theatre and Concerts
At the Manoel Opera House in Valletta, you can see ballet performances or hear concerts by the Manoel Symphony Orchestra and international soloists and groups throughout most of the year except for the hottest summer months. There are amateur dramatic societies that put on occasional plays in the theatre, and in the summer there are sometimes Shakespeare performances outdoors at San Anton Gardens. You can get details of current productions from the mini-guide, *What's On.*

Gozo has two big, elaborately decorated theatres, and there are a few plays and operas running throughout the winter season.

Cinema
There are several cinemas in Valletta and Sliema, and one in almost every village. Films are mostly shown in English, a few in Italian. Many are of the

sensational, "grade-B" quality. Opening hours vary.

Gozo has only a few cinemas, in Victoria, but each shows a different film every day through most of the year, except in July and August.

Dancing

There are no real floor-show nightclubs in Malta or Gozo, but some of the big hotels have live music for dinner dancing. A few restaurants offer barbecues, music and folklore dancing. There are various "Malta by Night" tours, folklore evenings, "Medieval Banquets" and similar evening excursions and entertainments.

Discotheque life is as lively as anywhere else, especially among the young. There are several discotheques around Malta, especially in Sliema and St. Julian's, and a few lively ones on Gozo. Some are even partially or totally outdoors, which is magnificent in the summer. Unfortunately for night crawlers, but fortunately for local inhabitants, discos close down at midnight to curb "noise pollution", though some clubs stay open later. All disco clubs are accessible to anybody with the money to pay.

Casino

Malta's modern casino, at Dragonara Point, St. George's Bay, attracts many fanatic or casual gamblers. You're advised to bring your passport the first time you play here—and only as much money as you're prepared to lose. The casino opens at 8 p.m. and closes well after midnight, depending on the action.

Dining out in Malta

The best of Maltese food is rich with hearty Mediterranean flavour and colour—juicy red tomatoes, gleaming onions, dark or light green peppers, tender squash or marrow, the freshest of fish, often with exotic names. Garlic, olive oil and herbs play an important part too, although the British with roasts or fish and chips and Italians with pasta and sauces have undoubtedly been the big influences. Maltese cooking does exist, and if you keep your eyes open, you'll spot a few authentic Maltese specialities on the menu.

Both Malta and Gozo have made an effort in the restaurant field, and you can eat well for a reasonable price, especially simple things like fresh *fettucini* or grilled swordfish with lemon. The Maltese bread—with a crisp brown crust and soft inside—is a real treat. On the other hand, what passes as "French" bread is a bland and rather tasteless roll.

As for the type of restaurants you choose, you'll find everything from the simple, neon-lit place (where you can usually eat for next to nothing) up to a vast outdoor garden or seaside terrace with candlelight at night and attentive service. Restaurants are classified into four grades by the government with the price ranging accordingly. Hours of serving are roughly the same as on the Continent: lunch 12 noon to 2 or 2.30 p.m. and dinner 7 to 10 p.m.

Breakfasts may be Continental or English-style (sausage, eggs and bacon).

Antipasti

You'll often see starters or hors d'oeuvres listed the Italian way. These may include slices of local pepper sausages, Parma ham *(prosciutto)* and melon, black or green olives, mixed little vegetable platters (as in Italy), shrimp cocktail or smoked salmon.

Soup and Pasta

The most frequent soup on the menu is *minestra*, a hearty vegetable concoction that is thicker than the Italian version *(minestrone)*, and made with just about everything in the kitchen garden: onion, potato, broad or haricot beans, cabbage, zucchini (baby marrow), pumpkin, tomatoes or tomato puree, and some pasta. It's a meal in itself! If you see fish soup, try it, especially if you like a highly seasoned flavour.

Fresh tomato soup is excellent, and menus often offer good consommé.

All kinds of pasta are popular with the Maltese, and very good. *Timpana*, if you can get it (usually only in a Maltese home), is a true Maltese dish to make you forget any diet: flaky pastry filled with macaroni, minced meat, onions, tomato puree, aubergines (eggplant), eggs and cheese, unmoulded and served in slices. A simpler version sometimes seen in small cafés is macaroni moulded with egg and cheese.

If you like Italian food, you can do almost as well as in Naples. Many restaurants have nearly all-Italian menus, so you can take along your Italian phrase book. Otherwise, menus usually appear in English, with occasionally a few French dishes listed in French.

You'll see all versions of Italian pasta, like *tortellini al sugo Bolognese* (little meat-filled pasta preparations with tomato-meat sauce), *tagliatelle alla crema* (flat noodles with cream), *vermicelli alle vongole* (tiny vermicelli with clams). Maltese *ravjul* is a tasty version of ricotta-stuffed ravioli. Many restaurants offer delicious *risotto* dishes, based on rice and cooked with various vegetables and sea-food.

Fish and Shellfish

Fish is top fare in Malta and it's treated with respect, which means flavour is enhanced, rather than being disguised with exotic sauces. *Lampuka* is Malta's "own" fish, and the season, beginning in late August and going through to November, is a big moment. The first day of *lampuki*-running, the fishermen raise their little triangular flags in salute. It is a firm-fleshed white fish, and may be served grilled, casseroled with wine and herbs, with piquant sauce, or in a kind of pie *(torta tal-lampuki)*, or pre-fried and cooked in a pastry shell with onion, tomatoes, cauliflower, spinach and perhaps olive oil and walnuts.

Octopus, squid and cuttlefish *(calamari)* are often eaten cold in salad, as a stew with curry flavour, or stuffed.

Fresh fish dishes usually include grilled swordfish, fried or grilled red mullet or *merluzzo*, tunny (tuna), *dentiċi* (dentex) or *ċerna* (grouper). Grouper may also be steamed whole and served in butter or in a piquant sauce. Any fish *alla Maltese* means served with a tomato and green pepper sauce. Fried scampi (prawns) are popular, and, as in most places in the world, lobster is prized and expensive.

Meat

Most restaurants offer international specialities, perhaps something like *filet de bœuf sauce béarnaise* (fillet of beef with *béarnaise* sauce); but watch for something typically Maltese such as *braġoli* or beef olives. These are a type of beef *paupiette* or roll stuffed with bacon, breadcrumbs, hard-boiled egg, parsley and a touch of garlic, fried, then simmered with onions and wine.

Beef or lamb dishes in Maltese homes are usually a kind of casserole in which the meat has been cooked with potatoes and onions. This is what roast beef "Maltese-style" means if you see it on the menu. Most island meat specialities don't appear on menus—things like braised pork, ox-tongue in a wine sauce or fricassee of meat balls with sweetbread or brains.

You'll often see good beef and veal on menus, Italian-style. *Filetto alla Meranese*, for example, is beef fillet wrapped in bacon and served in good brown sauce. *Vitello alla Marsala* would be veal scaloppini with Marsala wine sauce; veal

A refreshing breeze adds to the pleasure of dining out in Malta.

may also be breaded and deep-fried.

Leg of lamb or lamb chops are popular, and sometimes lamb is served shish kebab-style, on skewers.

The pork produced on Malta was renowned for its texture and flavour, but in 1979 a disease struck Maltese pigs, and they all had to be destroyed. Now new, uncontaminated pigs are being raised on Comino, and hopefully pork will soon be in circulation again.

Fenek (coniglio in Italian) means rabbit, and is a favourite sometimes served in restaurants—fried, stewed or casseroled with wine and garlic, curried, or as a delicious tart *(torta tal-fenek)* with pork, peas, tomatoes and spice.

When you're served country-raised chicken, you're in for a treat; it may be roasted, *alla diavola* or *diable* (grilled with shallot, mustard, breadcrumbs) or perhaps even *à la Kiev*—breast with a melting butter-herb filling that serves as the sauce.

Vegetables

There are always good, fresh vegetables available, no matter how bad the drought. The potatoes are delicious, whether sautéed, baked or as chips (French fries). Baby new potatoes in butter are a special treat. You'll have excellent mixed salads, perhaps creamed spinach or buttered beans *(fagioli).* And sometimes you can sample fried or ricotta-stuffed aubergines (eggplant) and baby marrow (zucchini) as well as stuffed tomatoes or green peppers.

Cheese and Dessert

Many restaurants serve excellent Italian cheese—Parmesan, Ricotta, Gorgonzola, Bel Paese —plus other imports like Gruyère, Cheddar and sometimes Roquefort. You might see the dry Maltese ewe cheese, deliciously spiked with peppercorns; another type, found in country towns, is aged in brine and capers. Perhaps the most common local sheep's milk cheese is called *gbejna.*

An ideal dessert is fruit: fresh figs, plums and peaches are juicy-sweet and abundant in summer. Tangerines and oranges are wonderful in the winter, and at various periods strawberries, melons and mulberries are available. The prickly pear is intriguing, but its seeds can be a nuisance.

The Maltese have a sweet tooth, so there's plenty of Italian-style, creamy ice-cream available everywhere in many flavours. Some sweet-shops **97** and restaurants sell fancy *semi-freddo* or semi-cold ice-cream-cake confections.

Restaurants usually serve some type of *gâteau* or *torta* (cakes made with chocolate, almonds, fruits and so on) and fruit tarts. Ricotta is sometimes used in sweet cheesecakes with fruit or combined with chocolate, cherries, sugar and almonds to fill little cornets called *kannoli tar-rikotta*.

Festivals bring their own sweets too. At Eastertime, you'll see *figolli* in the shops, delicious iced almond-lemon biscuits (cookies) cut in various shapes—men, women, or baskets. Shops display all kinds of iced cakes at all times of year, but especially flavoursome are sesame rings, macaroons and treacle rings. A favourite confection at carnival time is *prinjolata*, a mouth-watering combination of sponge fingers, butter cream and almonds or pine nuts, decorated with chocolate and cherries. During all *festi*, you'll see stands selling almond nougat and other sweets.

Snacks
Many little bars sell lunch or snack food—simple things like meat-filled pasties. *Pastizzi* is a Maltese speciality: a flaky puff-pastry turnover with a filling of ricotta, pea-and-onion or anchovy. You can also get various sandwiches: chicken, ham-and-cheese and so on.

If you make sandwiches for your picnic, do as the Maltese do: pack big pieces of the local bread or rolls with olives, tomato, onion, anchovies, hard-boiled egg, tuna and whatever else you can squeeze in, plus a generous sprinkling of olive oil. Hotels will sometimes provide a box-lunch for tourists taking a day-long excursion.

Drinks and Wine
Coffee, tea and all types of soft drink are readily available. *Kinnie* is the local non-alcoholic thirst-quencher, though its odd sweet taste does not appeal to most visitors. The usual alcoholic drinks are served almost everywhere, with gin-and-tonic or Scotch the perennial British favourites. Many types of beer are sold. The local lager, *Farson's Cisk* ("chisk") is good, and inexpensive.

You can purchase the best imported wines, but Malta and Gozo produce some unpretentious, appealing wines sold for a much lower price. Take care at first, they have a fairly high

No one claims the wine is world class, but it's tasty—and heady.

alcoholic content. Reds tend to be rather heavy and sometimes a bit sharp, and are best drunk slightly chilled. These include *Marsovin Special Reserve*, *Lachryma Vitis*, *La Valette* (considered the best), *Farmers* and *Festa.*

White wines, nicely balanced between dry and fruity qualities and drunk well-chilled, are quite refreshing. Brands sold are *Lachryma Vitis*, *Marsovin Special Reserve*, *Marsovin Sauterne* (very sweet, this one),

Farmers and *Festa.* Beware of the mild to drastic laxative effect a large quantity of these wines can produce in the uninitiated. The only rosé, rather sweet, is *Marsovin Verdala.*

Gozo produces fairly respectable wine, including *Velson's* red and white. The *Ġgantija* wines (red and white) are sweet, high in alcohol content, and have been known to produce excitable behaviour when drunk in quantity by non-Gozitans.

Read the Menu

The list below contains a selection of the words (Maltese, Italian and French) that you might come across on a Maltese menu.

abbachio, agnello, agneau	lamb
aċċola	amberjack (a fish)
aglio, ail	garlic
anitra, canard	duck
antipasto	starter (appetizer), hors d'œuvre
asparagi, asperges	asparagus
bistecca (alla boscaiola)	beefsteak (with wine-mushroom sauce)
boeuf, manzo	beef
braġoli, bragioli	beef olive *(paupiettes)*
brodu	clear consommé
calamari	squid
carciofi, qaqoċċ	artichoke
ċerna	grouper fish *(mérou)*
coniglio, lapin, fenek	rabbit
costata, costicine	chop, little chop
dentiċi, dentice	dentex (a fish)

dolce	sweet, dessert
espadon, pesce spada	swordfish
fagioli, fagiolini, haricots	beans
formaggio, fromage	cheese
frutta	fruit
funghi, champignons	mushrooms
gâteau	cake
ġbejna	Maltese sheep's milk cheese
homard, astice	lobster
insalata, salade	salad
lampuka	type of dolphin-fish special to Malta
melanzana	aubergine, eggplant
melone	melon
minestra	minestrone, thick vegetable soup
naranja	orange
pastizzi	turnover pastry with stuffing
patate, pommes de terre	potatoes
pesce, poisson	fish
piselli, petits pois	peas
prinjolata	special rich Maltese cake (for festivals)
prosciutto, jambon (e melone/ fichi) (avec melon/figues)	ham (with melon/figs)
riso, riz	rice
risotto (pescatora)	rice dish with other ingredients (with shellfish)
saltimbocca	veal scallops with ham and herbs
salsa	sauce
scaloppini, escalope de veau	veal scallop
scampi, crevette	shrimp, prawn
tagliatelli, pâtes	flat noodles
timpana	Maltese speciality of meat and cheese in a pastry case
torta	cake
tortellini	small, stuffed pasta
tonn, tonno, thon	tunny (tuna)
uove, œufs	eggs
vitello, veau	veal
vongole	clams
zuppa, soppa, soupe	soup
zucchini, qarabali, courgettes	baby marrows

How to Get There

While the types of fares and regulations described below were in force at the time of printing, it is advisable to check with a travel agent before finalizing holiday plans.

From Great Britain

BY AIR: Daily non-stop flights operate between London (Heathrow) and Malta throughout the year. Current fares on scheduled flights include first class, economy, economy night, and APEX (Advance Purchase Excursion). The APEX ticket is valid for a minimum stay of seven days (maximum three months) and must be booked and paid for at least one month before departure. No stopovers are permitted. Children ages 2 to 12 pay 50% of the APEX fare.

Charter Flights and Package Tours: Many cheap flights and packages are available, including inexpensive summer flights from Gatwick, Luton and provincial airports. Contact a reliable tour operator.

BY RAIL: The most direct route from London is Calais–Milan–Rome–Naples–Messina (short ferry ride)–Syracuse, then taking the ferry to Malta (service three times a week). Sleeping and dining cars are available on international trains as far as Naples; they are sometimes available as far as Sicily, but the service is considerably restricted and is less reliable. You may take your car on the train as far as Rome throughout the year; in summer, all the way to Villa San Giovanni (last stop on the Italian mainland).

A once-weekly car and passenger ferry links Naples with Malta.

BY ROAD: The quickest route is via Calais, Mt. Blanc Tunnel, Milan, Florence, Rome and Naples, then taking a ferry from Naples. A more scenic route goes by way of Calais, Rheims, Basle, through the Gotthard Pass to Milan, and down the Italian coast via Genoa to Naples or perhaps as far as Reggio di Calabria. Ferry service links this port with Malta (calling at Sicily) three times a week.

BY COACH: Europabus travels between London and Rome all year round. From April to October there are daily buses from Rome to Naples; here you could take the Malta ferry.

From North America

Though no direct flights link North America and Malta, there is daily connecting service to Malta (Luqa airport) from Chicago, Dallas/

Ft. Worth, Houston, and New York, as well as Montreal and Toronto. Connections are also available on specific days of the week from ten other major American cities, plus Edmonton and Vancouver in Canada.

In addition to first class and economy, the major carriers offer two special reduced-price fares (there are no youth fares to Malta at the moment). The APEX (Advance Purchase Excursion) fare must be reserved and paid for 21 days in advance of travel, and is valid for 14 to 45 days. During the peak season (June through August), this fare is somewhat higher. Stopovers are not allowed on the APEX fare, and there is a penalty for cancellation. Children (ages 2 through 11) fly for two-thirds of the adult APEX fare.

The Excursion fare (valid 14 to 60 days) has no advance ticketing requirements, cancellation penalties, or surcharges. This fare is more expensive during high season, May 15 to September 14. Children pay 50% of the adult Excursion rate.

At present, there are no package tours or charter flights available to Malta. Contact your nearest Tourist Information Office (see p. 124) for information on lodging possibilities in Malta (see also HOTELS AND ACCOMMODATION, pp. 115–116).

When to Go

Summer heat can be intense in Malta, especially when the sirocco blows in from Africa, raising the humidity. Temperatures are less extreme in the spring and early autumn, though nights can be on the cool side. Winters are usually rainy.

Average monthly air and water temperatures:

		J	F	M	A	M	J	J	A	S	O	N	D
Air temperature													
Max.	°F	63	64	68	72	78	85	92	92	86	82	74	67
	°C	17	18	20	22	26	29	33	33	30	28	23	19
Min.	°F	47	47	49	51	56	63	70	70	70	63	54	49
	°C	8	8	9	11	13	17	21	21	21	17	12	9
Water temperature													
	°F	58	58	58	59	64	70	75	78	77	74	67	61
	°C	14	14	14	15	18	21	24	26	25	23	19	16

Planning Your Budget

To give you an idea of what to expect, here's a list of average prices in Maltese pounds (£M). They can only be approximate, however; in Malta, as elsewhere, inflation is high.

Airport transfer. Taxi to Valletta £M 4.

Baby-sitters. £M 1 to 1.50 per hour.

Car hire (*per day* with unlimited mileage, high season). *Mini 1000* £M 7 for 1–3 days, £M 6.50 for 4–6 days, £M 6 for 7 days and over. *Ford Capri* £M 9 for 1–3 days, £M 8.50 for 4–6 days, £M 8 for 7 days and over. *Ford Granada* (automatic) £M 12 for 4–6 days, £M 11 for 7 days and over. (Officially, the daily tariff is £M 3.75 irrespective of make of car.)

Cigarettes. Maltese brands 30c per packet of 20, imported 54c and upwards.

Ferry to Gozo. From Sa Maison Pier, Pietà, return £M 1.30 per person, £M 3.50 per car.

Food and drinks. Set *meal* in medium-priced restaurant £M 0.50, bottle of local *wine* from £M 1.50, *soft drinks* 20c, *coffee* 15–20c.

Guides. £M 5–7 for 4 hours, £M 7–9 (plus lunch or compensation £M 2) for full day (8 hours).

Hairdressers. Woman's haircut £M 1–2, shampoo and set £M 2.50–3.50, shampoo and blow-dry £M 2–3. **Barbers:** haircut from 90c, cut and blow-dry £M 2.

Hotels (single room with breakfast [de luxe without]). *De luxe* £M 23 high season, £M 18 low season. *Class IA* £M 9, *Class IB* £M 8, *Class IIA* £M 6.55, *Class IIB* £M 6, *Class III* £M 4.60, *Class IV* £M 4.

Shopping bag. *Beef* £M 2 per kilo, *chicken* (frozen) £M 1 per kilo, *potatoes* 55c per kilo, *loaf of bread* 10–11c for 750 grams, *butter* 15c for 227 grams, *milk* 10c per bottle, local *wine* 30–90c per bottle, *whisky/gin* £M 4.20 per bottle.

Souvenirs. Set of three Maltese *lace doilies* £M 6.50, silver *cuff links* with Maltese cross £M 5–6, gold filigree *brooch* £M 30–50, silver filigree brooch £M 4–8.

Water sports. *Rowing boat* £M 2 per hour, sailing dinghy £M 3–4 per hour, *wind-surfer* £M 4–5 per hour, *water skiing* £M 5 for 15 minutes' lesson (or £M 2.50 every 5 minutes), *scuba diving* (boat dives) £M 6 per dive.

BLUEPRINT for a Perfect Trip

An A-Z Summary of Practical Information and Facts

Contents

A star (*) following an entry indicates that relevant prices are to be found on page 104.

All the information given here has been carefully checked, but changes occur rapidly and if readers should come across any errors, we would be glad to hear of them.

A **AIRPORT*.** The Maltese islands are served by Luqa airport, some 6 kilometres south of Valletta, a driving time of about 15 minutes. The airport has recently been enlarged to accommodate jumbo jets, and is used by Air Malta and some other international airlines. Customs formalities are fairly simple, though sometimes slow due to large crowds. There's a currency-exchange counter open 24 hours a day. The airport has an air-conditioned restaurant, a snack bar, bookstall and car hire desks. The small duty-free shop sells tobacco, perfume, wines and spirits. An Air Malta information counter helps with inquiries and problems. The airport post office is open Monday to Saturday from 7.30 a.m. to 7 p.m., Sundays and public holidays from 2 to 7 p.m.

Bus service to Valletta is infrequent, and the stop at least a 20-minute walk from the airport terminal building. Some hotels run an airport minibus service; alternatively, taxis are available. (Ask the price first; no matter what the "official" fare is supposed to be, taxi drivers charge according to what they think they can get.)

There's no airport on Gozo; see "Ferries" under TRANSPORT for how to get there.

On departure from Malta, you must buy a stamp, obtainable from the airport bookstall, in lieu of airport tax.

Note: Summer travellers are advised to reach the airport well in advance of the return flight. It is not unknown for certain airlines to overbook and "bump" passengers at the last minute.

Flight inquiries: tel. 622901
622915
22876

B **BICYCLE HIRE.** Cycling can be strenuous (particularly under the Maltese summer sun), but the islands' flat terrain and reasonable dimensions lend themselves admirably to the sport. Cycles can be rented for relatively little; in this way, you avoid traffic jams, parking problems and general harassment. For further details, consult the Tourist Organization (see TOURIST INFORMATION OFFICES).

CAMPING. There are no organized campsites on Malta and Gozo.

CAR HIRE*. See also Driving. Major international car hire firms operate in Malta, as do dozens of small free-lance agencies, some reliable, others less so. In any case, rental terms are reasonable, and tourists as a whole prefer hiring to bringing their own cars, or, alternatively, they take guided tours by bus or taxi. However, in peak tourist periods early booking is advisable. The smaller firms may try to hire out inadequate cars. Insist on a recent model.

To hire a car, you should have an international driving licence, and some companies may ask to see your passport. Most agencies set a minimum age for car hire at 25. Reputable firms accept major credit cards as payment, though some may ask for a cash deposit. The rates on page 104 include tax and third-party insurance.

And, before you actually set off, don't forget you're in a left-hand drive country...

Chauffeur-driven cars. This way of sightseeing is a lot more comfortable than driving yourself on the rather difficult roads—if you can afford it. The charge per hour is high. Some garages impose a minimum rental period of 8 hours. Taxis can also be hired by the hour, half day or day, with prices ranging wildly according to your bargaining skills.

CIGARETTES, CIGARS, TOBACCO*. Some international brands of cigarette are made locally. Maltese makes are less expensive than foreign ones. Major international brands of cigars and tobacco are also on sale.

Cigarettes and tobacco are available in many small shops with no special identification, except for a display which makes it clear they sell tobacco. Some shops may be marked "tobacconist".

CLOTHING. Light and loose cotton clothes are the best daytime items for the hot summer. Women usually prefer fullish skirts—cooler than slacks. Everyone should have a hat or scarf for protection from the sun, and comfortable rope- or rubber-soled shoes or sandals for sightseeing (different styles are available locally, though they're not exactly high fashion).

But heat doesn't mean you can go around half-dressed. The Maltese are on a campaign against unseemly dress in public places (bathing costume, bare midriff).

The strict Maltese Catholic ethic prohibits shorts, miniskirts, low-cut or shoulder-baring dresses while visiting churches. Women may be handed a scarf to cover shoulders and/or head.

Although bikinis are now a common sight at beaches, the topless look and nudity are not only out, but illegal, and you risk a fine or worse if you try.

In the evening, certain luxury hotels and the casino require jacket and tie for men; women may want one or two informal long dresses or skirts or dressy trouser-suit combinations. Take a jersey or a wrap for cooler evenings.

In winter, the climate demands light woollen clothing, jackets, jerseys, possibly a spring coat or a raincoat.

COMMUNICATIONS

Post offices. Postal service is generally quite efficient in Malta. The General Post Office at Auberge d'Italie in Merchants Street, Valletta, keeps the following hours:

Summer (June 16 to Sept. 30), 7.30 a.m. to 6 p.m., Monday–Saturday

Winter, 8 a.m. to 6.30 p.m., Monday–Saturday

Sundays and public holidays, 8 a.m. to 12 noon

Branch post offices are open from 7.30 a.m. to 12.45 p.m., Monday–Saturday all year round.

The Main Post Office of Gozo is at 129, Republic (Racecourse) Street, Victoria. Hours are:

Summer, 8 a.m. to 12.30 p.m., Monday–Friday, Saturday till 11 a.m.

Winter, 8 a.m. to 12.30 p.m. and 1.15 to 4 p.m., Monday–Friday, 8 to 11 a.m. on Saturdays

Stamps may also be bought at most hotels and at some tobacconists. Mailboxes are painted red; some date from the time of Queen Victoria, and have "VR" on them.

Poste restante (general delivery). If you wish to have your mail sent to you c/o poste restante, you should write ahead of time to warn the post office (address the letter to the Postmaster General, General Post Office, Valletta, Malta).

Telegrams. You can send telegrams from the Telemalta Corporation in St. John's Square, Valletta, from 7 a.m. to 7 p.m., Monday–Saturday (except on holidays), and at Luqa airport every day. Alternatively, the Main Telegraph Office (open 24 hours a day) is in St. George's Road, St. Julian's.

To phone in a local telegram, dial 98 on Malta and 556667 on Gozo.

Letter telegrams, or night letters (with minimum 22 words), are half the ordinary rate.

Telephone. Public telephone boxes, conveniently situated on many streets and squares, look like their British counterparts, but are painted blue. Information in the telephone directory is in Maltese and English. For local calls, you can usually dial direct from your hotel room by asking the operator for an open line. Some hotels allow non-guests to use their lobby phones.

Calls abroad can be dialled direct to Britain, France, Germany, Italy and Libya only. For other countries, dial 94 (894 from Gozo) to get the Overseas Telephone Exchange.

Hotels are authorized to add an extra charge for calls placed.

All outside calls from Gozo must be preceded by the number 8.

COMPLAINTS. If things go wrong, try complaining first to the owner or manager of the establishment. The friendly Maltese invariably try to set things right when you explain your problem. If you are still not satisfied (in the case of shops, restaurants, hotels, discos, etc.), you can then go to the National Tourist Organization (see TOURIST INFORMATION OFFICES). For hotels, rented flats and restaurants, contact the Hotels and Catering Establishments Board, at the same address as the Tourist Organization, but with phone number 23537.

If your problem is bad merchandise or car repairs, complain at once to the merchant or car hire firm. If this fails, go to the National Tourist Organization. Complaints made to the police will usually be referred back to the Tourist Organization or the Hotels and Catering Establishments Board.

CONVERTER CHARTS. The decimal system was adopted in 1972 for Maltese currency, and has already been well assimilated throughout the islands, though the occasional confusion can occur. Basically, metric weights and measures are familiar to young people (taught in schools), but far less so to many people over about 35.

Temperature

C **Length**

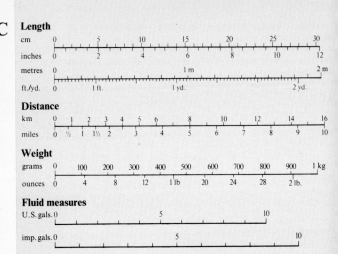

Distance

Weight

Fluid measures

COURTESIES. To help you meet the Maltese, there are no "official" organizations, but you really need no such help. The people are proud and dignified yet kind and friendly. If you want to enter into conversation, discuss the beauties of their islands. They may invite complete strangers around for a drink, or to share tea or coffee in a hotel or café. Whenever problems arise, whoever is around will try sincerely to help, whether locating an address, finding a telephone or getting your car repaired. Whether in shops or restaurants, on guided tours, at the beach or a swimming pool, it is easy to meet the Maltese. Young people also mix and meet at the many discotheques.

The islanders have the casual Mediterranean way of looking at things, and "tomorrow" or "later this afternoon" is just as good as "right now" for getting things done. So be insistent, while trying not to hurry them too much. They have a strict Catholic upbringing, and are usually very polite, even sometimes formal, on a person-to-person basis. They treat each other and strangers courteously, and expect the same treatment in return.

Nobody is going to ask you to speak a word of Maltese, but you will get amused and happy smiles if you try out *bonġu* ("good morning") and *bonswa* ("good evening"), *skużi* ("excuse me", pronounced just like in Italian) and *grazzi* ("thank you", almost like Italian). See also LANGUAGE.

CRIME and THEFT. Malta is still relatively crime-free compared with the rest of the world, and tourists are safe almost anywhere. But the incidence of theft is on the increase. It's wise policy to take the usual precautions: deposit your valuables in the hotel safe; if you've rented a flat, don't leave them in a conspicuous place. Lock your car as a matter of principle. Any loss or theft should be reported immediately to the nearest police station, and, if it happened at the hotel, to the hotel management.

The possession, use and distribution of drugs are criminal offences, punishable by fines and/or prison.

CUSTOMS and ENTRY REGULATIONS. See also DRIVING. For a stay of up to three months, a valid passport is sufficient for most visitors.

Here's what you can take into Malta duty free and, when returning home, into your own country:

Into:	Cigarettes	Cigars	Tobacco	Spirits	Wine
Malta	200	or	200 g. of other tobacco products*	¾ l. and	¾ l.
Australia	200	or 250 g. or	250 g.	1 l. or	1 l.
Canada	200	and 50 and	900 g.	1.1 l. or	1.1 l.
Eire	200	or 50 or	250 g.	1 l. and	2 l.
N. Zealand	200	or 50 or	½ lb.	1 qt. and	1 qt.
S. Africa	400	and 50 and	250 g.	1 l. and	1 l.
U.K.	200	or 50 or	250 g.	1 l. and	2 l.
U.S.A.	200	and 100 and	**	1 l. or	1 l.

* of which not more than 50 g. in loose tobacco
** a reasonable quantity

Currency restrictions. There's no limit on how much foreign currency a non-resident may bring into Malta (providing it's declared upon ar-

C rival), but you are entitled to import only £M 50 in local currency. Visitors may export a maximum of £M 25 in local currency, plus any remaining foreign currency of the sum they brought in and declared to customs upon arrival.

D **DRIVING IN MALTA.** If you're going to go to all the trouble of taking your car to Malta, you'll need

- your national driving licence (but if you hire a car, an international licence is required)
- car registration papers
- insurance coverage (the most common formula is the Green Card, an extension to your regular insurance, making it valid abroad)

Though there are practically no standard equipment requirements on Malta or Gozo, it's safe policy to use seat belts, and bring a red warning triangle for use in case of emergencies.

Driving conditions. Take care! is rule number one, especially if you're not used to driving on the left. After a bit of practice, you'll get the hang of it. The rules in general follow those in Great Britain: drive on the left, overtake on the right; in roundabouts (traffic circles), yield right-of-way to cars already in the roundabout circuit.

Speed limits are theoretically 40 kilometres per hour (25 mph) in built-up areas, 55 kph (34 mph) on the larger roads.

The best policy for visitors is to drive defensively, giving large berth to lorries (trucks) and buses, or precedence to aggressive-looking vehicles. Driving in Malta, and especially on Gozo, can be a trial for a newcomer used to order.

In the centre of Valletta, many streets are closed to cars, others are one-way, and the rest are usually clogged.

Road conditions. There are a few stretches of road big enough for four lanes. Both Malta's and Gozo's main central routes, though not always in good repair, are usually wide enough to accommodate two or three vehicles abreast. The roads often have potholes, sometimes repaired by hot tar and an amalgam of stones plus a fine dust topping. Smaller roads are sometimes very poor, and unless you're careful, you may get stuck on a road or country path that narrows down so much that you have to back out. It's best to use the horn when going around what look like sharp corners and hairpin turns, especially in small villages.

Parking is usually where you find it, though it is "prohibited" in many
places. But just be sure not to block anyone, or an exit. There are no

parking meters. If you put your car in a parking lot, give the attendant a small tip when you leave.

Traffic police. You don't often see them, but they do patrol roads in pairs, whether in cars or on motorcycles. You might see an occasional roadblock for identity checks if the police are looking for criminals.

Fuel and oil. Fuel is available in super (98 octane) and diesel. All service stations close on Sundays, so be sure not to run out of fuel on Saturday night.

Breakdowns. Towing and on-the-spot repairs are made by local garages, and spare parts can usually be found for most current makes of car. If you're renting your car, first call the hire firm who should be able to send help within the hour.

Accidents. In case of an accident, call the police immediately:

Malta, tel. 88, Gozo, tel. 556011

It is wiser not to move your vehicle until the police arrive, since accident claims are not usually settled unless the police make a report on the spot.

ELECTRIC CURRENT. Electric supply is universally 240-volt, 50-cycle A.C. The three-pronged British plugs and sockets are used. American visitors will need an adaptor.

EMBASSIES and HIGH COMMISSIONS

Australia	High Commission, Airways House, Gaiety Lane, Sliema; tel. 38201
Canada	Embassy (Italy), Via G. Battista De Rossi, 27, 00161 Rome; tel. 855393
New Zealand	Embassy (Italy), Via Zara, 28, 00198 Rome; tel. 8448663
United Kingdom	High Commission, 7, St. Anne Street, Floriana; tel. 21285
U.S.A.	Embassy, Development House, St. Anne Street, Floriana; tel. 623653/623216/620424

E **EMERGENCIES.** In case of accident or other emergencies, phone:

	Police	Ambulance	Fire
Malta	24001/2	96	99
Gozo	556011	96, or 556851	99
		(Craig Hospital)	

For traffic accidents, see under DRIVING.

G **GUIDES*.** The National Tourist Organization (see TOURIST INFORMA-
TION OFFICES) can provide you with qualified official guides who must
wear a red badge showing they have passed a strict comprehensive test
of history and languages. Your hotel can also find a guide for you. For
tours guides, tipping is included, but you might give a museum guide
a few cents.

H **HAIRDRESSERS*.** Malta's better hair stylists are generally well up
on the latest styles and cuts. If you're swimming and in the sun a lot,
it's a good idea to ask for a hair conditioner.

Some hairdressers are listed in the *What's On* guide. The bigger
hotels also have good hairdressing salons.

Hairdressers are usually tipped about 10 to 15%.

HEALTH and MEDICAL CARE. In this warm and humid climate, as
in many similar places, newcomers may contract "tourist's tummy",
often due to fatigue, too much sun and change of diet. Food and drink
are quite safe, but be sure fresh fruit and vegetables are washed.

The water is generally safe for drinking, but it is often unpalatable.
Do not drink water from fountains. Water in hotels and homes comes
straight from the "mains", and is therefore safe. Most mineral water,
at reasonable prices, is from Italy. The local brand, slightly bubbly, is
Farson's *San Michele*.

Don't quaff too much of the local wine—excellent but with potent
laxative effects for the unwary in the case of the cheap, common vari-
ety. If gastro-intestinal or other problems last more than a day or two,
see a doctor.

Beware of the sun, which is very powerful in the summer months.
Start with a sun-cream screen or complete-block (total) cream at first
and build up a tan gradually in small doses. The occasional salt tablet
doesn't do any harm when you're perspiring a lot.

There are plenty of insects in country areas around Malta and par-
114 ticularly on Gozo, especially in the hottest part of summer. But don't

worry, there are several sprays available in the shops if flies bother you. Small, invisible "nits" can leave itching bites; for these, use the insect repellent and itch-remedy creams obtainable at the pharmacy. The same goes for mosquitoes. If you should have mosquitoes in the room, buy an inexpensive coil called "moon tiger", which burns all night and keeps them away. Even more effective (more expensive as well) is the electric version of this. Both can be purchased at chemists.

Insurance. Malta has a reciprocal agreement with Great Britain, providing nearly the same free health care the British service offers. But if you come from elsewhere, make sure your health insurance policy covers accident or illness while on holiday—it's simply a wise precaution.

You may not get served in the hospital on silver platters as in the times of the knights, but medical equipment and treatment is usually of a reasonable standard, in spite of the fact that many Maltese doctors have left the island following a dispute with the Government in 1977. Doctors from other countries—Czechoslovakia, Pakistan, Libya, etc.—are serving with a few Maltese doctors in hospitals. General practitioners are all Maltese and well qualified.

If you need a doctor urgently, your hotel will help you find one; otherwise, the chemist can be of assistance. In an emergency, you can dial 96 on both Malta and Gozo, or:

Malta, St. Luke's Hospital (Gwardamanġa), tel. 621215

Gozo, Craig Hospital (Għajn Qatet Street, Victoria), tel. 556851

Pharmacies, clearly marked "Chemist" or "Pharmacy", are usually open during normal working and shopping hours. Duty pharmacies are listed in the local weekend newspapers.

HITCH-HIKING. It is permitted, though not common. If you do so, obey the normal common-sense rules. But it's much better to use the cheap and perfectly adequate bus service.

HOTELS and ACCOMMODATION*. See also YOUTH HOSTELS. Malta offers everything from luxury hotels to simple guesthouses. Around 100 hotels are rated according to comfort and amenities by the Hotels and Catering Establishments Board, which also puts out **115**

various brochures listing all details. The categories range from de luxe to class IV. The comforts you'll get in the luxury and often in the Ia and Ib categories usually include air conditioning, restaurant and bar, swimming pool, sometimes tennis court and private beach. Amenities diminish, of course, as categories go down; some class III and all class IV hotels, for example, have no lift (elevator). Brochures include all details.

It is imperative to book at the hotel of your choice well in advance if you plan to go during the crowded summer season or even early autumn.

Self-catering possibilities. Many people prefer to rent flats (apartments) or villas for their holidays. Prices and amenities vary. The National Tourist Organization brochure will give details of places listed for rent.

Note: Do not rent from somebody you encounter casually; some of these owners practise systematic rip-offs on unsuspecting tourists from abroad.

Health Farm. You might not think of Malta as a place to slim, but the Malta Health Farm offers what are termed "worthwhile results" within one to two weeks. A complete holiday complex, with all sporting and recreation facilities, in beautiful, warm surroundings makes it a "palatable", even an enjoyable experience. For further details, contact:

The Health Farm, Tarxien, Malta; tel. 823581. Cables: SAHHA Malta.

HOURS. Everything closes up for a few hours around lunchtime. The summer heat can be unbearable; so do as the locals do—relax until the cool of late afternoon.

Hours of opening vary wildly according to what the establishment is, whether government or private, what day of the week, which time of the year. The following is an indication of the general rules. (See also under COMMUNICATIONS and MONEY MATTERS.)

Government offices. Winter (Oct. 1 to June 15): 7.45 a.m. to 12.15 p.m. and 12.45 to 5.15 p.m., Monday to Friday. Summer: 7.30 a.m. to 1.30 p.m., Monday to Friday.

Offices and Businesses. 8.30 or 9 a.m. to 1 or 1.30 p.m. and 2.30 to 5.30 or 6 p.m. Most head or managing offices follow Government schedules.

Shopping hours are generally from 9 a.m. to 7 p.m. with a one- to three-hour break for lunch (usually closer to three), Monday to Saturday. Some establishments remain open during lunch.

The open-air market at St. John's Square, Valletta, operates until about noon, Monday to Saturday. On Sundays, a much larger morning market attracts crowds to St. John's Ditch just outside Valletta, a stone's throw from the bus terminus.

Museums. Most museums and sites are state-run and therefore have uniform hours all days except public holidays. Winter (Oct. 1 to June 15): 8.30 a.m. to 1 p.m. and 2 to 4.30 p.m. Summer: 8.30 a.m. to 1.30 p.m. Admission free on all Sundays.

Mdina Cathedral Museum. Winter (Oct. 1 to May 31): 9.30 a.m. to 1 p.m. and 2 to 5 p.m. Till 5.30 p.m. in summer. Closed public holidays and all Sundays except first Sunday of each month when hours are from 9.30 a.m. to 1 p.m. Admission free on first Sunday of the month.

Manoel Theatre. 10 a.m. to 12 noon and 3 to 4.30 p.m. From June 16 to September 30, mornings only.

Malta War Museum (in Fort St. Elmo). 8.30 a.m. to 1 p.m. and 2 to 4.30 p.m. except on public holidays.

Mediterranean Conference Centre. 9 a.m. to 12 noon on Tuesdays and Thursdays.

St. John's Co-Cathedral. 9 a.m. to 12.30 p.m. and 3 to 5.30 p.m., Monday to Saturday; from 9 a.m. to 1 p.m. on Sundays. The museum and oratory follow the same hours, but are only open on the first Sunday of the month; public holidays from 9 a.m. to 1 p.m.

LANGUAGE. You can get along fine if you speak English, since nearly every Maltese you'll encounter has a good to excellent command of it. Many speak Italian as well, and some speak French. However, the first language here is Maltese—both fascinating and quite incomprehensible to most foreigners. The pronunciation is especially difficult. Here is a key to some of the trickier consonants:

ċ – like *ch* in *ch*ild
g – like in *g*ood
ġ – like *j* in *j*ob
gh – silent
h – silent, except when preceded by gh
ħ – *h*

117

L

j – like *y* in *y*ear; **aj** is pronounced like *igh* in h*igh*; **ej**, like *ay* in s*ay*

q – like a very faint *kh*-sound, without English equivalent; a bit like cockney "ain't i*t*"

x – like *sh* in *sh*op

z – *ts*

ż – *z*

A few everyday expressions:

	Maltese	**pronunciation**
good morning	**bonġu**	BON-joo
good evening	**bonswa**	BON-swah
yes	**iva**	EE-vah
no	**le**	leh
please	**jekk jogħġbok**	yehck YOJ-bok
thank you	**grazzi**	GRAHT-see
excuse me	**skużi**	SKOO-zee
Where is…?	**Fejn hu…?**	fayn oo
right	**lemin**	LEH-meen
left	**xellug**	shehl-LOOG
straight ahead	**dritt il-quddiem**	drit il-KHOOD-dee-ehm
How much?	**Kemm?**	kehm

Numbers

0	**Xejn**	shayn
1	**Wieħed**	WEE-hehd
2	**Tnejn**	tnayn
3	**Tlieta**	TLEE-tah
4	**Erbgħa**	EHR-bah
5	**Ħamsa**	HUM-sah
6	**Sitta**	SIT-tah
7	**Sebgħa**	SEH-bah
8	**Tmienja**	TMEE-ehn-yah
9	**Disgħa**	DI-sah
10	**Għaxra**	AHSH-rah

For the most common town and site names, see under PLACE NAMES.

LAUNDRY and DRY-CLEANING. There are ample laundry and dry-cleaning services on both Malta and Gozo, and Malta has several self-service launderettes accessible to tourists during normal business hours. Laundry service takes about three days, as does dry-cleaning.

There are express one-day services, however, and top hotels offer both regular and same-day service, but same-day costs a lot more than the regular.

LOST PROPERTY. Check first where you think you lost the object; the Maltese people are, in general, scrupulously honest about other people's property. If you can't find the object, try at the nearest police station.

Lost children. Don't let young children out of your sight in crowded places (like the swarming main streets of Valletta). If a child is really missing, report it immediately to the police.

MALTA FOR CHILDREN. There aren't many special attractions for children on Malta, but they'll be happy all the same, especially on the beaches. The easy, sandy ones are wonderful for all ages, though you should keep an eye on very young children and toddlers, as there is not much in the way of life-guard service. The rocky beaches can be excellent for swimming and snorkelling or sailing for older children.

The *festi*, or religious festivals, are even more fun for children than for adults. They happen all summer long on weekends (the tourist office can give you a list of where and when). There are parades, perhaps little fairs, and on Saturday evenings the fireworks can be spectacular. Good displays to watch (from afar to avoid the crowd) include the St. George festival in Qormi and the St. Nicholas festival in Siġġiewi, both in late June on Malta, and the mid-August festival in Victoria, Gozo.

Children might like the *Imnarja*, or folklore festival, in Buskett Gardens. Also in late June, just after the folklore festival, is a donkey race at nearby Rabat. Other donkey and horse races to watch: in July, the feast of St. George in Victoria, Gozo, and in August, around the feast of St. Mary (Assumption) on both islands. Carnival parades take place on the second weekend of May. The regatta—boat races to celebrate Our Lady of Victories—is held on the Sunday nearest to September 8 in Valletta's Grand Harbour.

Other attractions for the young are the Għarb Museum and a little private collection in Żebbuġ, Gozo, both with amusing dioramas.

In St. Anton Gardens, Malta, a few animals and birds are on display.

Baby-sitting services are listed in the local papers and in the *What's On* guide.

M   **MAPS.** The tourist offices in Valletta and Victoria, Gozo, hand out a very basic map, which might also be available from your hotel. Otherwise, there's a good choice of maps at bookshops, hotel news-stands, etc.

MONEY MATTERS

Currency. Malta's monetary system is decimal. The *Maltese pound (£M)* is divided into 100 *cents (¢)*, the cent into 10 *mils (m)*.
   Notes: £M1, £M5 and £M10.
   Coins: 2 m, 3 m and 5 m and 1¢, 2¢, 5¢, 10¢, 25¢ and 50 ¢.
You won't usually be asked to give out mils, but you might get some back as change.
   Malta's gold and silver proof and brilliant uncirculated coins (£M25, £M50 and £M100 gold coins and £M1, £M2 and £M5 silver coins) can be purchased at the Malta Coins Distribution Centre, Central Bank of Malta, Castille Place, Valletta. Coins are sold at a premium. For currency restrictions, see under CUSTOMS AND ENTRY REGULATIONS.

Banking hours. In summer, hours are generally from 8 a.m. to 12 noon, Monday to Friday, till 11.30 a.m. on Saturdays; in winter, banks open and close half an hour later. These are branch office hours in most towns and villages in Malta. Certain banks have foreign-exchange facilities after normal hours. The commercial banking system is Government-controlled.

On Saturdays, banks will usually only change foreign cash up to the value of £M20. Many hotels give very low rates of exchange for **traveller's cheques**, so it's usually better to go to a bank. You'll need your passport when cashing traveller's cheques. **Credit cards** are widely accepted by better shops, hotels and restaurants in the bigger towns. Usually the symbols of the cards recognized for payment are on display. In shops, pay with Maltese currency or credit cards.

Prices are fairly reasonable when compared with the big continental cities. Food is inexpensive. Handicrafts (weaving, lace, knitting, pottery, glass, etc.) are good buys (see Shopping, p. 88). Prices are usually fixed, so bargaining is no good, but you can try haggling at small shops and street stands. Certain rates are listed on page 104 to give you an idea of what things cost.

N   **NEWSPAPERS and MAGAZINES.** All the English dailies and the *International Herald Tribune* are usually available in the afternoon of

the day of publication (the next day on Gozo) at most news-stands.
Two English-language papers are published daily, namely *The Times*
and the *Daily News*. There are two other English-language weeklies:
The Democrat published every Saturday and *The Sunday Times*.

The small fortnightly *What's On* guide gives a vast amount of information, everything from restaurants and cinemas to tips for the tourist.

PHOTOGRAPHY. There are many spectacular views to interest the
amateur or professional, especially where cliffs of pastel-coloured rock
tumble into the dark blue or turquoise sea, or in the small alleyways
and around the church squares.

Most well-known film brands are available, but not everywhere.
Valletta has several good photography shops. Super-8 camera film is
usually available, but you may have trouble finding 35-mm black and
white or special film like 200-ASA Ektachrome. Kodacolor and Agfacolor are easy to obtain, and slow-speed Kodachrome can be found
everywhere.

You may be able to get fast black-and-white development, but it is
rare. Colour film can take anything from a week to two or more,
depending on what type of film is used. So, unless you plan to stay
several weeks on Malta, it's best to have film developed at home.

The airport's X-ray machine does not ruin film, but for safety's sake,
put it in a bag to be examined separately by the checkers.

PLACE NAMES. See also LANGUAGE. The Maltese like to hear at
least their town names pronounced properly. So here's a list of the
main sites mentioned in this book.

Birżebbuġa	beer-zeeb-BOO-jah	Naxxar	NAHS-shahr
Borġ in-Nadur	borj in-nah-DOOR	Qala	KHAH-lah
Ġgantija	J'GAHN-tee-yah	Qawra	KHAW-rah
Għar Dalam	ahr DAH-lam	Qormi	KHOHR-mee
Għar Ħassan	ahr hahs-SAHN	Saqqajja	sahkh-KHIGH-
Għar Lapsi	ahr LAHP-see		yah
Għarb	ahrb	Siġġiewi	SEEJ-jee-eh-
Ħaġar Qim	hah-jahr-KHEEM		wee
Marsamxett	mahr-sahm-SHEHTT	Tarxien	TAHR-sheen
Marsaxlokk	mahr-sah-SHLOCK	Xagħra	SHAH-rah
Mdina	im-DEE-nah	Xlendi	SHLEHN-dee
Mġarr	im-JAHRR	Żebbuġ	ZEHB-booj
Mqabba	IM-khahb-bah	Żejtun	ZAY-toon

P

POLICE. Most towns have a police station, clearly marked and open 24 hours a day. All police officers, whether gazing at the traffic passing by or helping a tourist find his way, are dressed in casual cotton khaki uniforms in summer, black uniforms in winter, with visored hats. Police are very helpful on the Maltese islands, and are even responsible for delivering telegrams—in emergencies—to people in small towns who have no telephone.

Always contact the police immediately in case of a car accident (see under DRIVING).

PUBLIC HOLIDAYS. These are the official civic and religious holidays when banks, offices and shops are closed. Not listed are the numerous *festi* on various weekends in towns all over, though shops usually remain open on Saturdays.

January 1	New Year's Day	*August 15*	Assumption Day
March 31	National Day	*December 13*	Republic Day
May 1	May Day	*December 25*	Christmas Day
Movable date:		Good Friday	

R

RADIO and TV. Radio Malta broadcasts on three frequencies. One of them, Radio Malta International, puts on programmes in English and Italian.

On short-wave bands, reception of the BBC World Service is clear. Voice of America's programmes are also easily picked up.

Television Malta transmits about five hours of programmes in Maltese and English each evening, including both British and American features. English newscasts, preceded by a short roundup of general information for tourists, are put on at the end of regular broadcasts, about 10.30 p.m. or later. In Malta, you can also receive the two Italian national TV networks and a number of local Sicilian TV stations.

RELIGIOUS SERVICES. Malta is almost 100% Catholic. Most services are in Maltese. For non-Maltese Roman Catholics, St. Barbara Church on Republic Street, Valletta, celebrates mass in French, German and English at various times (see the local weekend newspapers or *What's On* guide). In St. Catherine's Church, Victory Square, Valletta, mass is said in Italian on Sunday at 11 a.m. St. Patrick's Church,

St. John Bosco Street, Sliema, celebrates mass in English (see *What's On* for times).

Other denominations have churches and services as well:

St. Paul's Anglican Cathedral, Independence Square, Valletta

Holy Trinity Anglican Church, Rodolphe Street, Sliema

St. Andrew's Church of Scotland, South Street, Valletta

Greek Orthodox Church, 83, Merchants Street, Valletta

Mosque, Corradino Hill, Paola

TIME DIFFERENCES. Malta follows Central European Time (GMT + 1), and in summer (March 31 till third Sunday in September) clocks are put one hour ahead (= GMT + 2).

Summer chart:

New York	London	**Valletta**	Johannesburg	Sydney	Auckland
6 a.m.	11 a.m.	**noon**	noon	8 p.m.	10 p.m.

Dial 95 for a time check.

TOILETS. There are few public conveniences and only in the larger towns, and the signs designating which is which ("ladies" or "gentlemen") are very subtle—sometimes you have to ask. If you see an attendant, you may give him or her a few cents. "Keep this place clean" cautions one sign in a Valletta convenience, "legal action will be taken".

TOURIST INFORMATION OFFICES. There is an Air Malta information desk at the airport, where they can advise about hotels and give other information.

The office to contact for detailed brochures on hotels, self-catering flats, etc., is the National Tourist Organization,

Harper Lane, Floriana; tel. 24444, telex 805 Holiday MT.

There is also a tourist information office at:

1, City Gate Arcade, Valletta; tel. 27747

where the staff give brochures and maps and will help with all problems except changing money, though they will tell you where to go for that.

T   In Gozo, go to the Department of Information, Main (It-Tokk) Square, Victoria; tel. 556454.

Tourist Organizations and information for Malta abroad:

Eire	Honorary Consul for Malta, 1, Upper Fitzwilliam Street, Dublin 2; tel. (01) 760-333
United Kingdom	Malta House, 24, Haymarket, London SW1 Y4DJ; tel. (01) 930-9851/5
U.S.A. and Canada	Maltese Consulate, 249 East 35th Street, New York, NY 10016; tel. (212) 725-2345/8 or: Embassy of Malta, 2017 Connecticut Avenue N.W., Washington D.C. 20008; tel. (202) 462-3611/2

TRANSPORT. See also CAR HIRE.

Bus services. Maltese and Gozitan towns are linked up by regular and efficient services, though in summer the buses get rather hot and crowded. You pay your fare to the driver. In Valletta, buses for all parts of the island leave from the Triton Fountain just outside City Gate. Destinations are indicated by numbers on the bus, and you can find out which number goes where by asking at your hotel desk, at the Tourist Office, or a bus driver.

In Victoria, Gozo, the main terminal is on Maingate Street.

Ferries. The only way to get to Gozo is by boat. Services between Malta and Gozo are frequent, but bad weather may render them unreliable. The car ferry *Għawdex* (pronounced "OW-dehsh") leaves each morning from Sa Maison Pier in Pietà Creek, Floriana, for the main Gozo harbour, Mġarr, a trip of 1 hour 15 minutes. It has ample space, a large, air-conditioned passenger lounge and café-restaurant.

Another car ferry, the *Melitaland,* is smaller and less expensive, but often crowded and uncomfortable in summer. It leaves from Ċirkewwa in north-west Malta for Mġarr several times a day, a 20-minute trip. A more luxurious ferryboat on this stretch is the *Mġarr*. From Ċirkewwa, it's quicker, but it means that if you start from Valletta or the airport, you have to drive to the other end of the island.

124   For car booking on Gozo ferries, telephone 603964.

On Comino, the island's one hotel runs a regular boat service to Marfa (on Malta) and back four times a day during the tourist season; call 573460 for further details.

In addition, travel agencies and cruise companies operate Comino cruises daily.

Taxis. They are clearly marked "taxi" and have red number plates. They also have meters, but these are rarely used—taxi drivers have a reputation of being somewhat tourist-minded on these basically honest islands. Agree on your price in advance. A trip from Luqa airport to Valletta or Sliema should cost no more than a 15-minute taxi ride would cost anywhere in southern Europe. Be wary at the airport and ferries. And if you leave from the hotel, ask the man at the desk to help you fix a fair price for your destination. Hotel receptionists will ring for taxis.

If you feel you've paid a correct fare, give a small tip (about 10%), especially in cases where the driver has been helpful in carrying your luggage.

Taxis are readily available at the airport, as well as at the main hotels, around tourist centres and at the ferry docks.

Horse-drawn cabs. First introduced in the 1850s, the *karrozzin* or horse-drawn cab has now become simply a leisurely way of visiting Valletta, Mdina and Sliema. For a rate definitely to be negotiated in advance, you can tour round for an hour (or more) the main sights of the towns. Pick up a cab at the Customs House or at Great Siege Square in Valletta; at St. Julian's outside the Malta Hilton; in Sliema, try at the harbour ferryboat terminus on the Promenade; and in Mdina, beside Bastion Square.

Water-taxis. Somewhat reminiscent of a gondola, the characteristic *dgħajsa* (pronounced "DIGH-sah") or water-taxi with its gay colours, plies the harbours of Malta's main ports. *Dgħajjes* can be hired (at rates to be negotiated) at the Customs House in Valletta and on the waterfronts at Senglea and Vittoriosa.

YOUTH HOSTELS. There are youth hostels in Senglea and Birżebbuġa. For information, contact the Malta Youth Hostels Association:

17, Tal-Borġ Street, Paola; tel. 29361

or NSTS—Student and Youth Travel:

220, St. Paul's Street, Valletta; tel. 624983/626628

Index

An asterisk (*) next to a page number indicates a map reference. For index to Practical Information, see page 105.

INDEX